MOSAICA PRESS

DOVID SOMMER

raising
a mensch

Practical Discussions and Inspiration
for the Family

BASED ON THE PARASHAH

Translated and adapted from
the *Chovas Ha'adam B'olamo* series: *Sugyas*
RABBI ZEV FESTINGER

Published by Mosaica Press, Inc.
www.mosaicapress.com
info@mosaicapress.com

In loving memory of our dear parents

LOUIS and ANNE PRICE

TEDDY and ROCHIE WEITZMAN

Dedicated by
HILTON AND RENÉ PRICE

In loving memory of our dear parents

ABE and MILLY SACHS

FREDY and ILSE SOMMER

Dedicated by
MARTIN AND MASHIE SOMMER

In honor of our dear parents

HILTON and RENÉ PRICE
MARTIN and MASHIE SOMMER

Dedicated by
DOVID AND CANDI SOMMER

In memory of my esteemed father

R' NOACH MOSHE zt"l
ben R' YITZCHAK ELCHANAN
HAKOHEN MELTZ

ר' נח משה זצ"ל בן ר' יצחק אלחנן הכהן מלץ

Trustworthy in his conduct and deeds,
pleasant to Hashem and pleasant to people,
always a smile on his face—
with these qualities, he influenced all those who knew him.

May his memory be for a blessing.

ט"ז שבט תשס"ב

תנצב"ה

Dedicated by his son
HILLEL
May he continue to spread and glorify the Torah
with ample resources and peace of mind.

On the occasion of the 90th birthday of

MRS. BLIMA NUDELMAN

Dedicated by

MENDY AND DENA NUDELMAN

Dedicated by

COLIN and LOREN GOLDSTEIN

In honor of

OUR DEAR CHILDREN and GRANDCHILDREN

Dedicated by
SHIMON AND RUCHAMA TRYFUS

In loving memory of

ARON ben CHAIM

YAAKOV AVRAHAM ben YESHAYAHU

ROCHEL NECHA bas SARAH

In honor of our dear friends

DOVID and CANDI SOMMER

May this *sefer* spread your light, love, and wisdom to its readers and be
a *zechus* for the Sommer family.

Rabbi Zev Leff

Rabbi of Moshav Matityahu
Rosh HaYeshiva—Yeshiva Gedola Matityahu

בס״ד

הרב זאב לף

מרא דאתרא מושב מתתיהו
ראש הישיבה—ישיבה גדולה מתתיהו

D.N. Modiin 71917   Tel: 08–976–1138 טל׳   Fax: 08–976–5326 פקס׳   71917 מודיעין .נ.ד

Dear Friends,

I have read portions of the book *Raising a Mensch* by Rabbi Dovid Sommer. The book is a translation of the Hebrew *Sugyos* (for children) from the *Chovos Adam B'olamo* series by Rabbi Zev Festinger. As the Hebrew version bears the approbations of various great Torah personalities, my approbation is unnecessary. However, I commend the translator for a quality presentation, producing a work that is written in a lucid, interesting, informative, and inspiring manner and is faithful to the content of the Hebrew version.

This book is a welcome addition to the English-speaking community that could not benefit from the Hebrew edition. It presents issues related to the various weekly Torah portions. The lessons are geared to children but can be enjoyed by adults as well. The lessons are instruction in proper character traits and behavior, presented with a Torah idea that is then applied to everyday living with questions for discussion and practical advice.

I recommend this work to all those whose *"mama lashon"* is English, even those who could understand the Hebrew version but reading it in English will be better understood. This work will definitely enhance children's and adults' sensitivity to issues of good character and behavior and engender a true Torah lifestyle.

May Hashem Yisborach bless the author and translator with life, health, and the wherewithal to continue to merit the community.

Sincerely,
With Torah blessings

Rabbi Zev Leff

Rav Moshe Samsonowitz
Menahel Ruchni
Simchas haTorah Kollel, Modi'in Ilit

BS"D 24 Sivan 5770-2010—edited 29 Elul 5778-2018

To my illustrious, beloved friend,
Rav Zev Festinger, shlita
You were appointed by Heaven to open a new window of opportunity for the general public, particularly avreichim and bnei Torah, for achieving character improvement in an orderly and systematic way.

The seforim that you have produced "Chovos haAdam b'Olamo", have become very popular in many yeshivos and homes, and the results speak for themselves.

The pleasant tone of your seforim, together with their pedagogic and galvanizing approach, inspires every person who comes in contact with them to want to read more and invest the effort to improve himself. Many groups have formed to work on themselves based on the series.

You are blessed with the talent to adapt the gedolei mussar's nuanced and lofty concepts into practical and doable concepts, especially due to the specific exercises you provide in the book.

It was my privilege to explore with you several points and sources for this greatly needed series.

• • •

We owe a debt of gratitude to Rav Sommer who undertook to translate the books to English.

This was a difficult challenge because of its unusual concepts and expressions. He has succeeded admirably in this task.

May your efforts to provide material and teach character improvement have a great benefit for our Jewish brothers!

May we merit to fulfill with all our heart "and you shall go in His ways", which indeed is your pure wish.

In faithful friendship,

Moshe Samsonowitz
Yerushalayim

Table of Contents

Sefer Vayikra

Sefer Bamidbar

Sefer Devarim

Acknowledgments

AT THE END OF every worthwhile project, it's tempting to stand back and say, "I did it!" But it simply isn't true. Both the Torah and life remind us that a person cannot accomplish alone. Let me begin by acknowledging everyone involved in my life in general and in this project specifically. Although I would like to thank every person by name and in detail, this is not possible due to lack of time and paper.

There are certain people, though, whom I feel truly obligated to mention.

To Rabbi Zev Festinger: As author of the original book in Hebrew called *Sugyos*, you worked meticulously and selflessly to create an incredible resource for parents and children. Thank you for investing so much time, energy, and passion into this and all the other books that you have written. May Hashem continue to give you all that you need to help others to reach their potential.

To Mosaica Press, and specifically Doron Kornbluth: You were excited about and believed in this project from the very first day we met. Your professionalism, creativity, and dedication are truly inspiring.

To my brother Ron: You visualized, initiated, and worked side by side with me to make this book go from a dream to what you now hold in your hands. *Yasher koach* for the teamwork.

To my extended family and friends: You have helped create and share the experiences that have been so enjoyable, powerful, and special. May we continue to share many *simchahs* together and in good health.

To my *rebbeim* and teachers: You helped me become the person I am today. I appreciate the ongoing wisdom, dedication, and belief in your communities and *talmidim*. May Hashem grant you all the resources you need to continue your incredible *avodas Hashem*.

To my parents and in-laws: You have always given of yourselves to do your best to raise us. Thank you for always putting so much into our family and showing us the way—back then and still today. May you merit to see and enjoy many generations of *ehrliche Yidden* with much *yiddishe nachas*, good health, and happiness.

To my wife and children: As Rabbi Akiva said about his wife: "Whatever I have is yours." I am forever indebted to you for all that you do for and with me, including making this book a reality. May we always grow to be true *ovdei Hashem*.

Finally, to Hashem, our ultimate Parent, Who loves and believes in each of us unconditionally: It was truly humbling to have this opportunity to learn and share the ideas in this book. May this and future projects enable fellow Jews to continue to raise true Torah *menschen* and be a constant source of pride to You.

Dovid Sommer
Ramat Beit Shemesh

Introduction

WHAT EXACTLY IS A MENSCH?

The word "mensch" is actually the Yiddish word for "a person." As we know, though, this term means a lot more than that. In fact, we automatically know a mensch when we meet him or her.

But what exactly is a mensch? Although everyone has their own personal definition, we can probably agree that a mensch is someone who does the right thing in the right way. Whenever anyone spends time with such a person, it's a most enjoyable experience. And why is that? Because he's got good *middos*.

A mensch is someone who knows and does the right thing—consistently. Whether he's by himself, engaged in something that's only between him and Hashem, or interacting with other people, he's doing what he should be doing. The Gemara (*Yoma* 86a) says that when a person learns Torah, serves *talmidei chachamim*, and deals pleasantly with people, he is beloved and praised by all who know him. In essence, he becomes a walking *kiddush Hashem* and source of pride to his parents, teachers, and Hashem.

But it's not just because he *happens* to be a nice guy. It's because he *became* a mensch. And that's why you picked up this book—because you know that raising a mensch is an *ongoing process*, not merely a gift.

So now the question is: How does a parent raise a child to be a mensch? As we know, it's not just another subject; it's one of the most important subjects in life. And that's why it's the subject of this book. Obviously, no book can cover everything on the subject, nor can it guarantee that one's children will become *menschen*. But as parents, we have the privilege and responsibility to do our best to help our children do their best. As it says in *Pirkei Avos* (2:16): "Rabbi Tarfon would say: 'You're not obligated to complete the work, and you're not exempt from doing it either.'"

Although addressing *all* the ideal *middos* comprehensively is beyond the scope of this book, it does deal with many of the core *middos*. If you take a look at the Table of Contents, you'll see that each chapter features a particular *middah*. This enables the family to explore and experience one *middah* at a time, and over time, your children will practice and internalize these *middos*. *B'ezras Hashem*, this book will help make the process more successful and more fun for the entire family. And Am Yisrael will merit to enjoy the next generation of *menschen*.

STYLE OF THIS BOOK

This book is the English version of the highly popular Hebrew sefer called *Sugyas*. All of the concepts were also explored at length in the series of Hebrew *sefarim* called *Chovas Adam b'Olamo*. Feel free to look at these *sefarim* for a more comprehensive analysis, as well as to practice the exercises to improve in the particular *middah* under discussion.

This book is divided into individual chapters. Each one addresses a specific *middah* or issue that's a critical part of being a mensch. It is also connected to a specific *parashah*, even though you don't have to follow according to the *parashah* of the week. The main idea is to expose children to the ideal *middos*, discuss them, and try to help as they internalize the messages.

The book has a style that is both user-friendly and hands-on because the ultimate goal is the practical application. Each *parashah* begins with a classic scenario that a child may typically experience, transitions into a *mussar* concept related to the *parashah*, then moves on to an inspirational story, and ends with a weekly exercise.

In each section, you'll see:

📖 A scenario—a practical situation with questions

📯 An insight and story—short and sweet

🎽 A challenge—weekly exercise

AT THE SHABBOS TABLE

The *Rosh* writes that there is a special mitzvah for a person to say *divrei Torah* during the meal at the Shabbos table. He learns this from the *pasuk*, "ודברת בם—And you should speak about them" (*Devarim* 6:7), explaining that this refers to discussing Torah ideas at your table (*Orchas Chaim*, section 44).

This is somewhat surprising, though. After all, isn't a person **always** obligated to learn Torah?! So what's the *chiddush* that one must also say *divrei Torah* at the table?

The great *mashgiach* of Kelm, Rabbi Daniel Movshovitz, *zt"l*, explains that the *Rosh* was referring to a specific type of *divrei Torah* during the meal, namely concepts that are appropriate for the level of the family members who are present. These would include subjects such as *emunah*, *bitachon*, *tikkun ha'middos*, etc. (as cited by Rav Shlomo Wolbe, *zt"l*, in his collection of essays on guidance for *chassanim*).

When a person eats, his heart is able to absorb and internalize these messages (*Chullin* 4). That's why it's extremely worthwhile to speak about these issues specifically during the meal.

THE GOAL

The purpose of this book is to give parents practical tools to draw young children into fascinating discussions about subjects on *middos* and *avodas Hashem* in the atmosphere of the Shabbos table. The scenarios are typical situations that the child experiences in day-to-day life. So when these issues are discussed at the Shabbos table, the child will then know how to behave when he encounters them in real life.

When the family discusses and then works on a certain *middah*, it helps everybody become more aware of it and, consequently, improve in that area. It also solidifies the family as a unit and strengthens their interpersonal relationships.

Many families have told us that the Hebrew *sefer* has had a powerful effect on the Shabbos atmosphere in their homes. By working together on the weekly exercise to improve on a certain *middah*, the family has experienced a dramatic change during the week that will hopefully provide lasting benefits.

Whether it's *chinuch*, *mussar*, *emunah*, or practically any other aspect of *avodas Hashem*, every good Jewish book repeats the following critical message. If we want to be successful, we have to **daven, daven, and daven**. That's ninety-nine percent of what we can do. After all, Hashem is our Partner in raising our children. All we need to do is ask for His help.

May we be able to raise our *menschen*, continue to grow in our *avodas Hashem*, and ultimately become like the "סולם מוצב ארצה וראשו מגיע השמימה—the ladder that is rooted firmly in the ground and whose top reaches up to the heavens."

PARASHAS BEREISHIS

Knocking before Entering

Fourteen-year-old Shimon returned home from davening Maariv. He opened the door, went inside, walked to the kitchen, and poured a glass of cold water for himself. He had absolutely no idea what was happening at that moment on the other side of the house…

Abba and Imma had gone to a wedding. Shimon's twelve-year-old sister had assured her parents that she would babysit the younger children and that they could go without worrying. "I'm very responsible and can take care of all the children until you return home," she said.

Imma made sure that the younger children were in bed and made supper for the two oldest children. Only after she saw that the baby had fallen asleep and that the other kids were lying in their beds did she feel comfortable to leave the house.

On her way out, she gave the following instructions to her daughter: "If the baby cries, give her a pacifier. She also has a bottle in the fridge, and you know how to warm it up.

"If one of the younger children wakes up, calm him down and

tell him that Abba and Imma will be back soon. Offer him a glass of water and tell him to go back to sleep in the meantime.

"Shimon went to daven. When he comes back in a few minutes, lock the door. You'll feel safer that way. Your supper is on the kitchen table, and after you eat, you can get ready for bed.

"If there's any problem, you can call me and Abba."

"There won't be any problem," said their oldest daughter confidently. And, sure enough, things went as smoothly as expected. Each of the children fell asleep quickly and everything seemed to be under control.

Until she heard noises…

Her mind started racing. I didn't hear anyone knock. Obviously, Shimon hasn't come home yet. So who is in the kitchen and moving things around? Maybe it's a thief…Help!

She tiptoed into the bedroom and closed the door quietly. Her heart was pounding. What do I do now?

Fortunately, the bedroom had a telephone. She dialed Abba's cell phone with trembling fingers. When he answered, she burst out crying. "Abba, there's a thief in the house!"

Abba tried to calm her down. But he was far away and she was alone at home, looking after the children—and now there was a thief in the kitchen!

She was hysterical and he felt so helpless. Even if he left the wedding immediately, he would only be able to get home in an hour. "Call the police!" begged his daughter. Abba was seriously thinking about doing this.

Suddenly, she noticed that the door handle of the bedroom was being pushed down. "Abba, he's coming in here!" she shrieked.

As she looked up, she saw Shimon walk in, smiling casually. "What happened? Why are you so frightened?" he asked in surprise. He couldn't understand why she was crying hysterically. It was so unlike her!

QUESTIONS FOR THE FAMILY

- Do you think that it's important to knock before entering?
- What problems can be caused if we don't knock?

In *Maseches Derech Eretz Rabba* (Chapter 5), Chazal tell us an important way to behave: "A person should not enter his friend's home unannounced."

Chazal add that this rule can be learned from this week's *parashah*—*parashas Bereishis*. Hashem didn't appear to Adam all of a sudden. Instead, Hashem stood at the entrance to Gan Eden and called out to Adam, as the *pasuk* says: "And Hashem Elokim called out to Adam and said to him, 'Where are you?'" (*Bereishis* 3:9).

We are supposed to try to act like Hashem, and so from here we learn that we are also commanded to adopt this *middah* of *derech eretz*. Chazal point out that this was the reason Yisro didn't arrive unannounced to visit Moshe, but rather let him know before. He sent a message to Moshe saying: "I, your father-in-law, Yisro, am coming to you, and your wife and two sons with her" (*Shemos* 18:6). The *Sforno* explains that Yisro notified Moshe in advance so that he would be able to prepare accommodation for them, as Chazal instructed: "Don't come into your home unannounced and certainly not your friend's home." It's *derech eretz*, the proper way to behave.

This should not only be done when first coming into the house, but also when one goes into any room in the house, especially the bathroom.

In this regard, the Gemara (*Niddah* 16b) says: "Rabbi Shimon Bar Yochai says, 'Hashem hates four actions…[one of them is] someone who enters his own home unannounced, and certainly his friend's home.'"

Rashi explains that this could result in an invasion of privacy.

The Gemara (*Kesubos* 62b) tells a story about Rabbi Chananya ben Chachinai who learned in Rabbi Akiva's yeshiva in B'nei Brak. He learned there for twelve years, during which time he didn't leave, even to return home. When one day he came home unannounced, his wife was so shocked that she couldn't say a word. She actually passed away from overexcitement. When Rabbi Chananya saw this, he pleaded with Hashem and said, "Master of the world! Is this the reward for this incredible woman, who waited for me for twelve years?!"

At that moment, a miracle occurred. Her soul returned to her body and she came back to life. Based on this incident, Rav said: "Don't enter the city unannounced and don't enter your home unannounced, and certainly not your friend's house unannounced."

CHALLENGE FOR THE WEEK

- Let's try to knock on the door before coming in.
- Be extra careful to knock before going into the bathroom.

Dealing with Peer Pressure

The wind was howling outside. But indoors, Shimon was very calm and content. He had managed to get dressed early, make his bed properly, and eat a bowl of cereal. He now had enough time to organize his new stamps.

Shimon took out his stamps and organized them in a row. He then selected the most valuable ones and inserted them into their appropriate places in his stamp album. He also wanted to sort out the other stamps, but he suddenly glanced at the clock and leaped out of his seat with a shout: "It's so late!"

He stuffed the stamps randomly into the album, grabbed his lunchbox, and was about to dash out the house when Imma stopped him.

"Wait a second, Shimon. You didn't put on your sweater yet!" she said.

Shimon glanced out the window. The sky was clear, without a trace of clouds. Why does anybody need a sweater on such a nice day like today? he wondered.

But Imma just stood there holding his blue sweater, hoping

that he would put it on. Shimon didn't reach out for it, though. That's because he was thinking about the incident with Gadi, his classmate, who had arrived at school a few days ago with a sweater. His friends had given him a "royal welcome."

"Hey, hey, hey! Look who arrived—a visitor from Siberia!"

"What happened to you? Did you catch a cold?"

"Ha ha ha. Look at him!"

"Are you feeling sick? Maybe you'd like a cup of tea?"

Oh no! I don't want to be laughed at by the whole class today. Why do I even need a sweater at all? thought Shimon.

"Imma, I'm not cold," insisted Shimon.

"It's not cold in the house," answered Imma. "But there's a strong wind outside."

The wind howled loudly but Shimon didn't hear it. All he heard was the teasing from his friends in class. He preferred to leave the sweater at home and freeze the entire day. As long as he wouldn't be like Gadi—standing all alone and embarrassed while all the boys made fun of him.

QUESTIONS FOR THE FAMILY

- Have you ever not taken a sweater because you're afraid of what others will say?
- Are there other things that you do (or don't do) because you're worried about what others will say?
- How can we stop worrying about what others think and just do what we need to?

In this week's *parashah*, *Parashas Noach*, it speaks about Noach building the *teivah* (ark). Without a doubt, there were many who mocked him:

"Which flood are you talking about?"

"You're making up nonsense. Obviously, a flood won't happen!"

"And even if there will be a flood, you won't manage to complete the *teivah*."

"And how exactly will you be able to fit all the animals into one ark? There are so many animals! Don't forget that there are 120 types of vultures—and hundreds of thousands of other animals!"

"Even if you do build it, we won't let you go into it. We'll make sure that you drown with the rest of us."

As time passed, the pressure on Noach kept increasing.

"Where's the flood that you promised? An entire year has passed and nothing's happened!" they taunted.

Another year passed. And then another. Already twenty years had passed. Everybody laughed at Noach.

Even Noach was beginning to have doubts. He thought about the *yetzer hara's* challenging questions: *Maybe they're right? Perhaps I didn't hear exactly what Hashem said? Maybe I didn't understand Him correctly?*

But Noach remained strong against everyone else. Noach kept doing what he needed to do and wasn't influenced by what was going on around him. Everybody around him was corrupt. He was under intense pressure, but he didn't care about them. He didn't give in to their demands and he did what he had to do.

We deal with the same type of challenges today.

A number of years ago, a researcher got together a group of people and told them he wanted to test their eyesight. He showed them some lines on a large board and asked them to identify the lines, which were equal in length. The task was fairly simple and they answered without a problem.

But then the researcher invited some others to "join in" a repeat of the experiment. These newcomers weren't actually *participating* in the experiment but rather *cooperating* with the researcher. And instead of testing how well they could see, the real goal of the experiment was to learn about peer pressure.

The researcher showed the lines to all the people and each person had a turn to answer. In the beginning, the people who were cooperating in the first exercise gave the correct answer. But in later exercises, they gave the completely wrong answer, calmly and confidently. The real participants in the experiment became confused but gave the exact same *incorrect* answer as everybody else.

Then the researcher shared the truth with the participants. Some of the people said that they knew that the answer was incorrect but felt uncomfortable in front of the other people and as a result gave the incorrect answer. Others said that they knew the correct answer but began to doubt themselves when they saw that everyone gave a different answer. They rationalized that the other people may have had more information and perhaps knew better than they did so they changed their minds. When the people from the third group (who also answered incorrectly) were questioned, they claimed that they really did believe that these were the correct answers.

From this experiment, we see that sometimes a person may give in to peer pressure without even realizing that his entire perspective has become distorted!

In fact, the *Rambam* (*Hilchos De'os Perek* 6) warns us about peer pressure:

> It is human nature for a person's opinions and actions to be influenced by his friends; he behaves like those around him. A person must therefore constantly associate with tzaddikim and talmidei chachamim so that he will learn from their actions. Similarly, he should distance himself from corrupt people so that he doesn't learn from their ways. This is what Shlomo HaMelech meant when he said, "The one who accompanies wise people will become wise and the companion of fools will suffer misery."

How should one deal with peer pressure?

The *Yesod V'Shoresh Ha'Avodah* (*Sha'ar* 1, *Perek* 1) suggests the following creative technique:

> *Imagine that all the people around you are animals. Would you be embarrassed if a frog would laugh at you for wearing a sweater and tell all his fellow frogs: "Look at this funny creature. He's some kind of weird animal that walks around with two legs, and he's got a sweater too!"*

A *chassan* and *kallah* were once going down the street. The *chassan* was riding on a donkey while the *kallah* was walking next to him. Some people passed by and commented, "What a mean person! He's riding on a donkey and leaves his wife to walk. Doesn't he care about his wife?"

The man heard what they said, got down from the donkey and let his wife ride instead. They went a little further, when a group of people saw them and remarked, "Look at this chutzpah! She's riding on the donkey and her husband has to walk."

The man heard this, took his wife down from the donkey, and they both continued walking next to the donkey. Once again, people passed by and said, "Look at these two silly people. They have a donkey, but both of them are walking!"

The couple then decided that they should ride on the donkey together. A group of people walked by and said, "Such cruel people. Both of them are so heavy and are sitting on such a thin, scrawny donkey!" With no other alternative, they got down from the donkey and lifted it onto their shoulders! A few people saw them and said to each other, "Look! Isn't that ridiculous?!"

The moral of the story: Someone who always decides how to behave based on what others will say will eventually lose their ability to think clearly.

CHALLENGE FOR THE WEEK

- Let's try to beat the fear of being embarrassed, using the above suggestions.
- Let's do the mitzvos—including the mitzvah of honoring parents—even if we're concerned that people might laugh!

Every Step to Do a Mitzvah Counts

Shimon dragged his feet slowly. The walk home at the end of the day was always so difficult and tiring. He walked slowly with the sun beating down on him. But even the most frustrating things have to come to an end, and now the end was in sight: home! What a pity, though, that his home was on the top floor of the building. Eventually, he finished going up the last two floors, thirty-six steps to be precise, opened the door, and flopped down on the sofa. "Hello—I'm back!" he said.

The sofa was where everybody sat and recovered from the trek home. That's where Shimon sat, enjoying the comfy softness of the big cushions, browsing through the youth newspaper and reading the latest comics section with total fascination.

Then he spotted the Lego blocks on the floor. Who left them lying on the floor like that? Somebody could step on them or trip on them!

Shimon sat down and started sorting out the different Lego pieces. He organized them according to color, sorted out the people, and set aside the special pieces. Great, now he could begin building and playing. What fun! Soon he was so busy with his Lego that he forgot about everything else. That's why he didn't hear that Imma had already called him three times.

All of a sudden, he heard Imma's voice, "Shimo-on!" She was standing right next to him. "Didn't you hear me?"

"Yes," he smiled, somewhat embarrassed, and stopped playing with the Lego. "What?"

"Please go to the store quickly and buy milk, eight yogurts, and a tray of eggs. I need these items for supper."

Shimon looked at the Lego sadly. He was right in the middle of having such a fun time. Right now, all he really wanted was to keep playing.

Imma gave him some money. "Shimon, I really need you to go, please."

Shimon, however, did not feel like going out at that moment at all. The walk there was okay—it was downhill. But to come back up that difficult hill afterward, with a heavy grocery bag in one hand and a tray of eggs in the other hand? Oh no! That definitely didn't interest him. He had hardly managed to get home from school and now he had to do this backbreaking journey again!

"Soon, Imma, in a minute. I'm just in the middle of playing," he mumbled. He picked up a Lego piece and started building. As he played, he thought to himself: Really, why specifically me? I just arrived home and I should go out again already?! It's not fair! Maybe Yossi can go? Maybe Chavi? Why me?

Once again, he was completely engrossed in playing, not noticing the look of disappointment on Imma's face.

QUESTIONS FOR THE FAMILY

- Do these situations also happen to you? Give examples.
- Were you ever able to overcome this challenge? How?

This week's *parashah, Parashas Lech Lecha,* tells us that after Pharaoh kidnapped and then returned Sarah, he sent her and Avraham away, as the Torah says: "And Pharaoh instructed the people with regard to him, and they sent away: him, his wife and everything that they owned" (*Bereishis* 12:20).

The Gemara (*Sotah* 46b) says: "Rabbi Yehoshua ben Levi said, 'As a reward for the four steps that Pharaoh accompanied Avraham, Pharaoh was allowed to enslave Avraham's descendants for four hundred years.'"

The *Maharsha* asks: "Wasn't the slavery already decreed at the *bris bein ha'besarim* when Avraham asked, 'How will I know?' and not because of the four steps that Pharaoh took?"

He answers: At the *bris bein ha'besarim,* it wasn't mentioned *by whom* the Jews would be enslaved. In the merit of the four steps that Pharaoh took, he earned the right for them to be enslaved *by him.*

Let's think about it. For every step that a person takes to do a mitzvah, he gets so much reward. Let's imagine how many steps are involved and how much reward there will be when our parents ask us to clean our room.

Avraham also received an incredible amount of reward when he left Charan and headed toward Eretz Yisrael to fulfill Hashem's command of "לֶךְ לְךָ—You should go." He received reward for every single step (*Midrash, Bereishis Rabbah* 39:9).

The *Peleh Yoetz* (*Erech: Hachanah*) writes that his teacher, Rabbi Avraham HaLevi, would spend considerable effort shopping for Shabbos because of the reward for every step.

The concept of reward for every step we take toward a mitzvah is one of Hashem's wonderful acts of kindness because He wants to give us so much reward! Let's try to remember that all our steps are recorded in Heaven and that angels are created from them.

Here are two stories about the incredible reward for the effort involved in doing a mitzvah.

There was a certain Jew who would clean the town shul. After he passed away, he went up to be judged by the Heavenly court. They began to weigh his mitzvos and aveiros on the scales. Black angels, produced by his aveiros, and white angels, produced by his mitzvos, came. All of them sat on the scales and eventually the scales balanced exactly in the middle. They didn't know what to do with this Jew. On the one hand, he could not be allowed into Gan Eden. On the other hand, he couldn't be sent to Gehinnom.

All of a sudden, they heard strange noises. Lots of angels, in the shape of shoes, started arriving and climbing onto the scales. These were all the angels that were made by all the steps that he took to pick up all the papers and trash that people had dropped in the shul. An angel was created from every step! Because there were so many of these angels, the Heavenly court ruled that he could go to Gan Eden.

Two wealthy people were once walking down the street. They saw a poor person begging for tzedakah on the other side of the street. The first wealthy person ran over to give him tzedakah. The second gave him the same amount, but waited for the poor person to come to him.

After they passed away, the two wealthy people met before the Heavenly court. After weighing up the mitzvos against the aveiros of the two people, the defending angel yelled, "Wait! There's more reward for the first wealthy person." And then they saw wagonloads full of reward for the steps that the wealthy person took when he ran from where he was to where the poor person was standing. These were added to his scale of merits. The other wealthy person, though, who didn't move and gave from where he was standing, didn't get such a special "delivery."

CHALLENGE FOR THE WEEK

When our parents ask us to do something, let's go and do it with *simchah*.

Choosing to Do Chessed

Shimon turned the page and discovered that the story had come to an end. In just two-and-a-half hours, he had finished the entire mystery novel that he had brought home that day from the library. He stretched and then stood up. After all, he had sat for so long without moving. The book had been fascinating! He closed the book, put it on the shelf, and went to the kitchen. After several hours of reading, he was a bit hungry.

Shimon stopped at the entrance to the kitchen and stared with shock at the unexpected chaos. Leftover sandwiches on the table, an open container of chocolate spread with brown marks all around, a bottle of ketchup with its reddish liquid slowly oozing out, dirty plates on the table and on the floor, cutlery on the counter and chair.

What's going on here? thought Shimon.

Oh, yeah. Now he remembered. Imma had told him something while he was totally engrossed in the part of the book about the kidnapping by the Iranians and their accomplices. What did she say? That she was hurrying. That she had to go out somewhere. Obviously, this was the reason why things were in such an unusual mess.

His mother, otherwise known as "Mrs. Neat and Tidy," never ever left her kitchen like this! She must have had no choice. She must have had to leave suddenly, without even having time to put the lid back on the container of cheese and put it in the fridge.

Shimon was still standing at the entrance to the kitchen. All of a sudden, he felt a strong desire to clean up a little. After all, what needed to be done? Basically: Cover the spreads and put them back in their place, stack the dirty dishes in the sink, throw the dry pieces of bread away, and sweep a little. Imma would be so excited to find a neat kitchen when she came back.

It would be a lot of work, though. Covering each container and putting it back in its place, bending down and picking up the cutlery that was stuck to the floor, collecting all the plates and dry pieces of bread, touching everyone's leftovers, and having to put it all in the trash. No! Absolutely not! He didn't feel like doing that. The desire to help began to fade away. The truth was that nobody had asked him to do it and he didn't have to. Imma didn't tell him to clean up. Nothing bad would happen if it would all stay like that until she came back.

On the other hand, Imma would be so delighted if he would clean up around here. Shimon leaned against the kitchen door. The mixed feelings bounced back and forth in his heart: I don't have to!...But it's the right thing to do...It's difficult, though...It's so worthwhile...

QUESTIONS FOR THE FAMILY

- Do these situations also happen to you? Give some examples.
- Can you remember examples of *chessed* that you did voluntarily?
- Can you think of ways to do *chessed* without even being asked?

When a person is sick, he usually lies in bed and doesn't have the strength to do anything. This week's *parashah*, *Parashas Vayeira*, tells us about Avraham, who was sick on the third day after having his *bris*. Avraham was a very old man and was extremely weak. But instead of lying in bed, he went outside to look for an opportunity to do *chessed*. From Avraham Avinu, we can learn about the importance of doing *chessed* proactively.

Some children tidy their rooms even when their parents don't ask them to. They also take the trash out before they're asked. When they notice children who don't have anyone to play with, they volunteer to play with them. They also offer to study with friends who need help preparing for a test. Some also sometimes go to their parents and ask, "What can I do to help?"

There is a story about the holy Rebbe Yehoshua of Belz, *zt"l*, who was seen on Yom Kippur afternoon walking back and forth among the many Chassidim who would come to spend the *Yamim Nora'im* with him. He would keep looking into their eyes. Nobody knew why until one time a person was about to faint from hunger. The Rebbe went up to him, took some cake out of his own pocket and gave it to the man to eat so that he wouldn't get sick. At that moment, everybody understood the rationale for the Rebbe's behavior. The Rebbe planned this *chessed* and kept the cake in his pocket in case this situation would arise.

CHALLENGE FOR THE WEEK

This week, let's try to do *chessed* without being asked.

PARASHAS CHAYEI SARAH

Saying Thank You to Teachers

Today's lesson was so interesting! The rebbi brought a lot of miniature sukkahs to demonstrate all the different examples that feature in the Mishnah. The students sat there fascinated, eagerly touching the tiny walls, examining the tiny schach, and admiring the delicate decorations that hung in the sukkahs. The rebbi passed the various models around the class so that they could take a good look at everything that they had learned. It was really fun!

It was not surprising that the students went to the rebbi at the end of class and thanked him with broad smiles. "Thank you—that was amazing!" they exclaimed.

Shimon, like everybody else, also thanked the rebbi. He, too, had enjoyed the amazing lesson. But at the end of the next lesson, which was just like any other lesson, he was very surprised to see his friend Yehudah go up to the rebbi and warmly thank him.

Shimon followed him around curiously. What was he planning on doing later on that day? Sure enough, at the end of the math lesson, Yehudah also went to the rebbi and said thank you. Shimon couldn't control himself. He ran after Yehudah and asked him, "What's going on here?"

"What?" wondered Yehudah.

"Why did you thank the rebbi?"

"Why not? He taught me something that I didn't know before. Because of him, I now know how to multiply fractions. That's why I thanked him."

Shimon frowned at him. "You actually like to multiply fractions?!"

"Definitely not!" smiled Yehudah. "But I didn't know how to do them until now."

"I don't understand," argued Shimon. "It's his job to teach the material to you. So why do you even need to thank him?"

"It is his job," agreed Yehudah. "Nevertheless, when the rebbi teaches me something, I feel obligated to thank him."

"Wait a second," challenged Shimon. "You mean to tell me that if my mother makes a Shabbos meal for me, then I should say thank you to her?"

"Yes."

"But she made the meal for herself too, not just for me!"

"True, but she also made it for you, so she deserves to be thanked. It's very important to show appreciation."

"It's not surprising that you're called Yehudah," laughed Shimon. "You're a professional at thanking!"

- Do you also say thank you to any of your teachers?
- Why should students thank their teachers?
- Who else should we thank?

This week's *parashah*, *Parashas Chayei Sarah*, tells us that Eliezer, Avraham's servant, was sent to find a wife for Yitzchak.

He thanks Hashem twice:

1. After he finds Rivkah, the *pasuk* says: "And the man bent down and bowed to Hashem. And he said, 'Blessed is Hashem, the G-d of Avraham my master, Who did not withhold His kindness and truth from my master. Hashem guided me on the way to my master's family'" (*Bereishis* 24:27).
2. When Lavan and Besuel allow him to take Rivkah, he gives thanks again as it says: "And he bowed down on the ground to Hashem" (*Bereishis* 24:52).

It seems difficult to understand. Why did Eliezer thank Hashem? Wasn't the *chessed* done to Avraham, who needed a wife for his son? This can be answered as follows: Eliezer also benefited from the quick *shidduch* because he did not have to continue searching. As a result, he too was very appreciative.

The story is told about a person who worked in a certain factory. He would greet the guard with a smile when he arrived every morning. And when he left every evening, he would say thank you to the guard on his way out. One day something very scary happened. When everybody left the factory at the end of the day, this specific worker stayed behind to organize something in the walk-in safe. Suddenly, the door of the safe closed behind him and he couldn't get out. He realized that he would die soon because the air in the safe was running out. He banged and banged on the door, but nobody heard because the other workers had already left. The guard, who was used to being thanked each time the man came and went, wondered why this person had not left the factory yet. He decided to go look for him. When he went into the factory, he heard the banging, opened the door for him, and saved his life.

CHALLENGE FOR THE WEEK
This week, let's try to thank one of our teachers.

PARASHAS TOLDOS

Saying "I Don't Know"

The Gemara shiur continued as usual. Shimon tried very hard to understand what the rebbi was saying. The rebbi was talking about two different opinions and explained each opinion separately. Shimon thought that he was starting to understand. However, when the rebbi started speaking about the differences between the two opinions, everything became mixed up in his head. Completely.

Perhaps because he had given a sigh of frustration. Or maybe because he had a confused look on his face. Either way, the rebbi turned to him at that moment and asked, "Shimon, did you understand the argument between Abaye and Rava?"

All eyes turned in his direction. Shimon didn't know what to do. Should he really announce in front of everyone that he didn't understand?

He nodded his head to show that everything was all okay. The rebbi then asked, "Is there anybody who didn't understand?"

No one raised their hand. Shimon was glad that he'd hidden the truth from the rebbi. If he would have admitted that he

didn't understand, he would have really embarrassed himself. Imagine—the only kid in the class who didn't understand!

As the lesson continued, though, Shimon was no longer glad. The rebbi did not repeat his previous explanation. However, everything that he taught was based on that initial argument. Shimon felt like he was getting more and more lost in the details of the question.

At the end of the lesson, Shimon put up his hand and asked if he could ask something. The rebbi gave permission, so Shimon stood up and asked his question. It was a really good question. The rebbi listened and was very impressed.

"What a great question!" he said when Shimon finished speaking. "In fact, it's a fantastic question! And you know what? I don't have an answer for you at the moment. I'll have to look up the various commentaries and give you an answer tomorrow, bli neder."

Shimon was shocked. The rebbi had been in the same uncomfortable situation—he didn't know what to answer—but he wasn't embarrassed to admit it! Now Shimon was upset that he hadn't told the rebbi how confused he was about the argument in the Gemara.

Maybe, just maybe, he could muster up the courage to go to the rebbi during recess and ask for an explanation.

QUESTIONS FOR THE FAMILY

- Were you ever too embarrassed to say "I don't know"?
- Have you heard adults saying "I don't know"?

In this week's *parashah*, *Parashas Toldos*, it says: "And Yitzchak sent Yaakov, and he went to Padan Aram to Lavan HaArami, [who was] the son of Besuel, [and] the brother of Rivkah, the mother of Yaakov and Eisav" (*Bereishis* 28:5).

Rashi's words on this *pasuk* are astonishing: "I don't know what this is teaching us."

There are quite a few places where Rashi writes that he doesn't know what the true meaning is. It seems strange. Why does Rashi write that he doesn't know? If he doesn't know, then wouldn't it be better to not say anything at all?!

The reason Rashi says he doesn't know is to show the importance of humility.

Following are two stories that highlight this idea.

> When the Mussar movement began, there were those who protested. The main concern was that this was a revolutionary movement that had suddenly appeared. Who knew what it could lead to? Eventually, everyone admitted that this movement was extremely important and even the Torah leaders who had initially opposed it retracted their views.
>
> When the great Rabbi Yisrael Salanter, zt"l, was in Vilna, he was asked to give some shiurim. Many people attended the shiurim and Rabbi Yisrael Salanter amazed all the people who were in the beis midrash with his breadth of knowledge and brilliance. Among those who attended these shiurim was a sharp-minded genius who wanted to minimize their powerful impact. He would constantly try to find a problem with Rabbi Salanter's ideas, using not-so-well-known sources in the Gemara. Rabbi Yisrael, however, with his incredible brilliance, always knew how to respond to this individual.
>
> One time, the genius asked an extremely difficult question during the shiur. Rabbi Yisrael listened, thought, and

immediately admitted that this question presented a difficulty on what he had said. He left the podium and stepped down from the stage. A few days later, he told his students that when he heard the question, he had thought of several answers that would have definitely been accepted by the genius and the audience. However, since he knew that these answers weren't actually correct and that the person who asked the question was correct, he left the stage.

Rabbi Yisrael then said, "Don't think that it was easy for me to admit this. I could have rationalized for various reasons: the honor of the Torah, the effect on those who were present, etc. Because these reasons were very believable, I could have allowed myself to simply dismiss the question. Nevertheless, I reprimanded myself as follows: 'Yisrael, Yisrael. You're somebody who learns mussar!' Then and there, I left the stage."

When the great gaon, the Beis HaLevi, was appointed as the rabbi of Brisk, everyone knew that he was one of the leading Torah authorities of the generation. However, after he became the rabbi and was presented with a halachic question, he analyzed it and answered, "I don't know." The people who asked the question were very surprised but remained silent. When another question was brought to him, he looked at it and replied that he didn't know. As the astonishment increased, so did the disappointment. They had been certain that they had found a leading Torah sage, but he didn't seem to know how to give simple halachic rulings! A third question was given to him, and again, he answered that he didn't know what the law was. This incident was too much for everyone to accept.

The leaders of the community organized a meeting to discuss the matter. They decided that their rabbi was probably an unbelievable genius in analyzing Talmudic issues and worthy of the position of Rosh Yeshiva. But as a community rabbi, he was an absolute failure. They chose a group of people who went to inform him about their decision. He listened to their claim, smiled, and said, "Rabbis, don't worry. I know how to give a halachic ruling. I just wanted to teach you, as well as myself, that if it happens to be that I don't know the answer, I won't be afraid to say, 'I don't know.'"

CHALLENGE FOR THE WEEK

If we don't understand something, let's try not to be embarrassed. Instead, we should say that we don't understand.

PARASHAS VAYEITZEI

Not Embarrassing Other People

A trip! How exciting!

Shimon was one of the first to get to school that morning. It was the best to arrive early on a day like this. This way, he could choose his seat and schmooze with his friends about the bus, the much-awaited hike, the great weather, and most importantly, the snacks.

Shimon had a full backpack stuffed with packets of chips in three different flavors, candies in different shapes and colors, lots of sour sticks, special chocolates, juice, and chocolate milk. The teacher had also said to bring two meals, so Shimon brought long baguettes crammed with tasty foods that he liked. All these supplies were squeezed into the bulging backpack.

He waited impatiently for the moment when the conversation would turn to the topic of snacks, because he would be able to show off all the goodies that he had brought with him. In the meantime, the children discussed whether a security guard

38 • *Raising a Mensch*

would come with them, and that the tour guide had better be really cool so that the trip would be the best ever.

What a pity they didn't allow us to bring cameras on the trip, thought Shimon, while he was half-listening to his friends' discussion about water hikes and climbing mountains. He personally didn't like hiking for miles and miles. He enjoyed other aspects of the trip, like the treats and photos. If they'd have allowed cameras on the trip, he could have shown off his new digital camera with all its neat features to his friends.

All of a sudden, he heard a whisper next to him. "Whew! I'm so glad they didn't allow anyone to bring cameras." Shimon looked sideways and saw Eli standing there. Eli noticed that Shimon was looking at him, and added, "We don't have a camera at home." He didn't say a word after that.

Eli had a thin, simple knapsack. It looked so different from Shimon's new one, which was bulging at the seams. Shimon wondered what happened to all of Eli's treats. Why didn't he buy any treats? Not even one?!

There may have been a small treat inside the pathetic-looking knapsack. But anybody could tell that there wasn't even a tenth of what Shimon had crammed into his.

Right then, the children finally started talking about the treats that they had brought. Great, this was the moment he had waited for! Shimon wanted to unzip his bag and show his friends all the goodies that he had schlepped along for the trip. But something stopped him…

How would Eli feel if he saw how much Shimon had brought, while his own bag was so empty? Even if none of his friends noticed how little Eli had brought with him, what would happen when the kids started showing off all their treats that they bought for the trip? Maybe Eli's parents didn't have money to buy so many treats? Maybe they could hardly manage to pay the full price of the trip?

QUESTIONS FOR THE FAMILY

- Should Shimon show his treats to his friends or not?
- Has a similar situation ever happened to you? How did you deal with it?

This week's *parashah*, *Parashas Vayeitzei*, talks about Rachel giving the secret codes to her sister. She knew that by doing this, she would probably lose her right to be the wife of Yaakov, and as a result she would not get the opportunity to have the twelve tribes come from her. Nevertheless, she decided that saving her sister from embarrassment was more important than her own future.

As the Midrash (introduction to *Eichah Rabbah*) says:

> *Rachel stood up in front of Hakadosh Baruch Hu and said: "Ribbono shel Olam, it's clear and obvious to You that Your servant Yaakov loved me more and worked for my father for seven years to marry me. When he finished those seven years and the time came for us to get married, my father wanted to switch me with my sister. This situation was very stressful for me because I knew about the plan. I let my husband know about it and gave him a secret code to tell the difference between me and my sister so that my father couldn't make the switch. But then I regretted it, put aside my dreams, and had pity on my sister so that she shouldn't be disgraced. That evening, they switched my sister for me, and I gave her all the codes that I had given to my husband, so that he would think that she was me..."*

In the end, Rachel was greatly rewarded for her selfless deed. Not only did she *not* lose out, but she actually merited having children *because* of this deed (Rashi on *Bereishis* 32:22).

There is an amazing story that the *Sdei Chemed* told about himself:

When I was a young avreich, I studied in a kollel. I was very diligent and really learned a lot. One of the kollel members, who was jealous of me, came up with a spiteful plan to get me in trouble.

He bribed the person who cleaned the kollel to say that he saw me stealing money from other people. The cleaner agreed and spread this rumor about me. A large crowd gathered around me and accused me of being a hypocrite. They embarrassed me and called me names. It was a huge chillul Hashem. I couldn't handle the embarrassment and had to run away.

The rosh kollel didn't believe the cleaner's story and fired him from his job.

When the cleaner ran out of money, he came to me and begged me to forgive him for the terrible injustice that he caused me. He promised me that he would share the truth with everybody and admit that the whole story was made up. He said that he would tell everybody that one of the avreichim bribed him to spread the false accusation about me. Since the cleaner was unemployed, he also begged me to help him to convince the rosh kollel to give him back his job once he could prove that I was innocent.

*At that moment, I was in a difficult situation. On the one hand, I was very excited about the long-awaited opportunity to clear my name from the terrible lie and get everything back to normal. However, a different approach also came to mind. After all, the chillul Hashem had already occurred. If the true story would come out now, then there would be **another** chillul Hashem due to the shameful behavior of the avreich. It would also cause him incredible humiliation. Maybe it would be better to continue suffering my own shame in silence until the uproar subsides, I thought; anything to avoid creating a new commotion. This predicament was extremely challenging. The* *thoughts kept racing around in my head. I changed my mind every minute. At last, I decided to tell the cleaner: "I agree to try to convince the rosh kollel to give your job back to you. But you are not allowed to tell anyone about the whole issue of the bribe and false accusation."*

When I made this difficult decision, which had the potential to jeopardize my future in the Torah world, I experienced an incredible revelation of wisdom. I was rewarded with unbelievable siyata d'Shmaya, which has made me who I am today.

CHALLENGE FOR THE WEEK

- Let's try to control ourselves and not embarrass other people in any way.
- Don't ask others how high they scored on their test.
- Also, don't bring so many treats to class if you know there may be someone who doesn't have any. Instead of boasting or laughing at him, help him.

Being Satisfied with What We Have

For whatever reason, dinner never works out well. Shimon really doesn't understand why. He does know that every time that he wants rice, his mother makes noodles. And on the day that he's in the mood for noodles, that's exactly when his mother makes potatoes.

He groans. "Oh no, why potatoes? I wanted noodles!" He doesn't understand why Abba is not happy with him and why Imma looks angry. What did he do? After all, he just said that he wants to eat something different.

The issue of seating is also a problem. He likes to sit on the chair next to the wall but somebody else grabs that place every time. Shimon gets angry, argues, and demands that the other person give the favorite seat to him. Usually, his siblings don't give in. Shimon then tries to get to that chair first and grab the spot, but they still keep irritating him. One brother sometimes stands on his foot. Every now and again, his younger sister

splashes her soup on him. And by the time his plate reaches him, the food is a bit cold. The truth is that he is sometimes too hot (under the collar) anyway.

In fact, things don't go smoothly at the Shabbos meals either. Shimon always asks to sit next to Abba, but his brothers don't usually let him have that place. What's strange is that even when Abba decides that Shimon can sit next to him, Shimon is usually still unhappy and decides to sit right next to Imma.

Strange, isn't it?

QUESTIONS FOR THE FAMILY

- Do you also behave like this sometimes?
- How would you explain Shimon's problem?

This week's *parashah, Parashas Vayishlach,* talks about how Yaakov got ready to meet with the wicked Eisav who wanted to kill him. When Yaakov and Eisav met, Eisav said, "I have plenty." But even though he was in charge of four hundred men and was known as a very important person, he wasn't satisfied. His words implied that although he didn't lack anything, it still wasn't enough for him. Yaakov was the exact opposite. He said, "I have everything." Even though he didn't have every single thing in the world, he still felt he had everything he needed.

Also, it says that a person dies without getting *even half* of what he wanted in life (*Koheles Rabbah* 3:13). Human nature is that if a person doesn't work on improving himself, he will always want more. If he has one hundred, he wants two hundred.

Chazal (*Avos* 4:1) taught us: "Who is the wealthy person? The person who is happy with what he has."

A child who always complains will never be happy. Sometimes, it may *look* like the child is happy because he got what he wanted. For example, he wanted to sit next to his father so he cried until he was allowed to sit next to his father. But in the end, he won't be happy. Why not?

The answer is that the child will only be happy *at that moment*. But it probably won't take long for him to start complaining and being upset about other things that he doesn't like.

This attitude can also happen with food. Even though a child doesn't have to eat every type of food that he doesn't like, it's not good to complain all the time. It just makes this bad habit more difficult to change. Even if he gets what he wants, he'll still find a problem that something's not yummy or enjoyable.

That's why it's a good idea to sometimes eat foods that one doesn't enjoy so much, as well as to stop complaining all the time…

The gaon Rabbi Eliyahu Lopian, *zt"l*, once asked a question about the wording of the *pasuk*, "And those who seek out Hashem will *not lack* any good" (*Tehillim* 34:11). Why isn't it written as follows: "And those who seek Hashem will *receive* all that is good"?

He answered with the following metaphor. A person went to visit his friend. The friend said to him, "Come. I want to show you my medicine cabinet. It's got all types of medications, including some very expensive ones that were sent from abroad. Nobody around here has as big a collection of medicines as I do!" Afterward, he asked the visitor, "And where is *your* medicine cabinet?" He answered him, "I am healthy, *baruch Hashem*, and I don't need all these medicines. In fact, I'm glad that I don't need any medications and I don't feel that I'm lacking any of them either."

Rabbi Eliyahu Lopian explains the above *pasuk* as follows: Those who seek Hashem don't need to *get* everything that is good because they're not lacking anything. They're already satisfied with what they have.

There was once a family who went on a day trip to the zoo. When they arrived home that evening, the mother asked them how they enjoyed the family outing.

One child said, "It was a lot of fun. We saw a lot of animals, including elephants, lions, monkeys, and zebras. It was a little hot, though, but it wasn't that bad because you let us wash our faces with water and then you bought ice pops for all of us. Even though it was very crowded, especially when they fed the elephants, the main thing was that I managed to see a lot of animals. The zoo was so big and we didn't get to see everything, but *b'ezras Hashem*, we'll finish seeing everything next time we go to the zoo."

However, the story of the second child was quite different. "I was so bored. What's so interesting about elephants, lions, monkeys, and zebras?! We walked so much and I really didn't enjoy the heat. Even though you let us wash our faces with water, it still didn't help for that long. And then when you gave us ice pops, mine melted and made my hands sticky. I really didn't like that. Also, the zoo was so crowded that it just wasn't fun to be there. We didn't even manage to see everything at the zoo. The whole trip just wasn't worth it!"

Both kids went on the exact same trip. But they described it so differently because they *looked* at it so differently. This is known as perspective; one boy had the perspective of "being happy with what one has," while the other did not.

CHALLENGE FOR THE WEEK

Let's try to be happy with what we have and eat whatever Imma serves us, without asking for anything else and without arguing about where we want to sit.

PARASHAS VAYEISHEV

Doing What We're Asked to Do

Shimon came home from the library very excited. He had managed to get the latest book!

Many kids had their eyes set on the most recent best seller that was hot off the printing press. He didn't stand much of a chance, but much to his surprise, the librarian decided that he should get it and wrote his name down for the book.

Shimon hurried home, holding the novel tightly in his hand. The picture on the front cover alone was enough to entice a person to read the contents...

He walked into the house, mumbled a quick hello, and stretched out on the sofa. He opened the book to the first page and was "gone" in an instant. He was now part of the story—in a cold, far-away city, a small child among strangers, desperately trying to find his father. But his father had disappeared and now he had to deal with some dangerous people. He became very scared when he heard that they were planning to blow up the city.

"Shimon!" called Imma. In that split second, her voice had interrupted and ripped him away from the terrifying plot. He lifted his eyes off the printed page with great difficulty and turned to his mother. She looked at him and said, "Shimon, please go the grocery store and buy two pounds of tomatoes."

What?! He should go out now and leave the hero of the story just like that—in the middle of such an exciting part?!

"In a little while," pleaded Shimon and looked back into the book. "I'll just finish the chapter."

Imma agreed and Shimon continued reading. His hero was hiding from the criminals, but the hiding place wasn't safe enough. Soon they would discover him…

A half hour later, Imma came back. "Shimon!" she repeated. "I'm still waiting. Leave the book for a minute and run to the grocery store."

But Shimon couldn't. The bad guys were about to catch him! How could he worry about getting tomatoes now? "In a little while, Imma, I'm in the middle of such an exciting part…"

QUESTIONS FOR THE FAMILY

- Does this also happen to you sometimes?
- What should Shimon have done?

When Yosef was sent by his father to check up on his brothers who were looking after the sheep in Shechem, the Torah tells us that he met a "man." This man was actually the angel known as Gavriel. Yosef asked him where his brothers were. The man told him, "They already left here because I heard them saying, 'Let's go to Dosan'" (*Bereishis* 37:17).

Rashi explains that the angel tried to warn Yosef not to go to his brothers, who were plotting against him. When the angel said, "They have already left here," he was hinting to Yosef that his brothers no longer thought of him as their brother. And when the angel quoted them as saying, "Let's go to Dosan," he meant that they would no longer treat him with love and respect. But Yosef still went to look for them because that is what his father told him to do.

From this incident, we learn that it is important to fulfill the mitzvah of honoring one's parents, even when it may be difficult.

But the Torah also highlights another important detail.

When Yaakov tells Yosef to go and see how his brothers are doing, Yosef says to him, "I am ready" (*Bereishis* 37:13), as if to say, "I am prepared to do whatever you want, Abba. Not in a minute, and not when I've finished reading the end of the chapter, but right now."

This is how we should honor our parents.

The *Yehudi HaKadosh* (from Peshischa) and his students were busy learning and came across a very difficult topic. The *tzaddik* was deeply involved in his learning and didn't notice anything else going on around him. During the entire time, his students sat around him and waited for their teacher to continue the lesson, but it was taking him a long time to look into the issue. All of a sudden, one of the students felt very hungry. He said to himself, "The *rebbi* will obviously still be thinking about it for a while. In the meantime, I can hurry home and have something to eat."

With this thought in mind, he hurried home, ate something, and was about to go back to the *beis midrash*. He was already on the doorstep when he heard his mother's voice. "Son, please could you go up to the attic and bring down a bundle of hay? As you know, I can't climb up to the attic, and I really need the hay now."

"But, Imma," the son responded, "I have to go back to the *beis midrash* right away. The *rebbi* is about to finish analyzing the issue and is going to start explaining!"

"Okay, my son," said the mother understandingly and let out a sigh. "It's better that you go back to your learning. Forgive me for asking. But what can I do? I need your help sometimes." A tear rolled down her cheek. "It's not easy being a widow…"

While thinking about these words, the boy left the house and started walking toward the *beis midrash*. All of a sudden, though, he stopped. "What am I learning for?" he asked himself. "Is it so that I can learn and know even more? What will that help if I don't practice it? After all, the whole purpose of learning is in order to keep what I learned, including the mitzvah of honoring parents. I'd better hurry home and do what my mother wanted!" He turned around and went back home. He climbed up to the attic and searched around until he found the bundle of hay.

"Imma, here is the hay that you asked for," he said, as he handed over the bundle to his mother, his eyes lowered in shame. "Please forgive me for not doing what you wanted right away." His mother's face lit up and she smiled broadly. "Thank you so much, my son. Now, run back to your learning. I hope that you didn't miss out on any of your *rebbi*'s insights," she said. Feeling much better about the situation, the boy ran back to the *beis midrash*.

"Please, Hashem," he whispered. "I hope I didn't miss out on anything that my *rebbi* said. Please make sure that I won't be late." With trembling hands, he opened the door of the *beis midrash*. Inside, the room was totally silent. The *Yehudi HaKadosh* was still completely involved in his learning. But when the door opened, the *tzaddik* lifted his head up from the book, and a smile spread across his holy face. He got up from his seat and turned toward the student standing at the entrance.

"When you came in," explained the *Yehudi HaKadosh*, "I saw Abaye, the great sage in the Gemara, walk in with you. He came and answered the difficult question that I was struggling with for such a long time. So tell me, how did you deserve to have such an important person come with you?" The boy then quietly explained what had happened to him earlier. "I realized that I made a mistake," he finished off, "so I returned home and did what my mother wanted."

The *tzaddik* turned to his students. "Now I know why your friend deserved to be accompanied by Abaye. Abaye was an orphan, with no father or mother, so he couldn't ever do the mitzvah of honoring one's parents. Since he passed away, he comes to those people who keep the incredible mitzvah of honoring one's father and mother." In fact, his name is an abbreviation of the words, "Because of you, the orphan will be taken care of" (in Hebrew: אביי = אשר בך ירוחם יתום).

(From *Ma'aseihem Shel Tzaddikim*)

CHALLENGE FOR THE WEEK

This week, let's try to do whatever our parents ask—right away.

Thanking Hashem for the Small Things Too

Shimon lay in bed and felt very sad. His throat infection wasn't going away. He'd had a fever for three days already. He'd been taking antibiotics for the last two days, but the fever had still not gone down. He was shivering all over, his throat was aching, and he'd had enough of drinking tea the whole day.

The telephone rang and Imma walked in with the cordless phone. "It's your friend," she said and handed him the phone.

It was Gadi. He wanted to know how his friend was feeling. Shimon was glad to be able to share the news about his bad throat infection.

Seconds later, Yehudah called. He also wanted to know how Shimon was feeling and when he would return to school.

Shimon was wiped out from these phone conversations but at least his mood had improved. It was nice to know that his friends had not forgotten him.

But then he had another bad bout of that irritating cough. Now his throat was on fire. Shimon moaned and Imma rushed to make him a cup of tea—the eighth that day! When she came back, she reminded him, "You can thank Hashem that at least you have friends."

Friends? wondered Shimon. Everybody has friends! Does a person have to say thanks for that? A person thanks Hashem for the big things, like miracles. Do I really have to be grateful that I have two hands, two feet, and a nose? Or that my hair is brown or even for a new shirt that I got? Of course not! Only if something really amazing happens, like if a car almost hits me. Or if all of a sudden, my throat infection would disappear, my fever would drop, and it wouldn't hurt at all. You only need to thank Hashem for those types of things!

Is that really true?

QUESTIONS FOR THE FAMILY

- Do you think that a person should thank Hashem for the small things too?
- Why?

On Chanukah, we thank and praise Hashem for all the miracles that He did for us. It's easy to thank Hashem for the miracle of Chanukah, because that miracle really was incredible and supernatural: a small group of Jews beat the mighty Greek empire!

But many miracles also happen to us every day that we don't even notice. And we *also* have to be grateful for the fact that we're healthy, we're able to learn Torah, we have friends, we have wonderful parents, we have so many talents…

We really need every single thing that Hashem so kindly gives us.

And when we don't have everything that we usually have, that's then we feel that we're missing something—and maybe even like we are suffering. We see from this that we have to thank Hashem for every good thing, no matter how small. Also, when we get into the habit of thanking Hashem for the small acts of kindness, then we get better at practicing the attribute of gratitude.

Once, there was a boy called Daniel. Daniel grew up in his grandmother's house and hardly remembered his parents. He was only three years old when his parents passed away in a terrible car accident. His grandmother was the only relative that he had. The social workers didn't want the elderly grandmother to be responsible for the poor little boy. "It was only a few months ago that you lost your husband, and now your son and daughter-in-law," they told her. "How will you manage to raise a small child who requires so much energy?"

But the grandmother was determined. "I don't have time to think about what I've lost. I have to focus on what I've still got," she said. And sure enough, she was awarded custody of Daniel. He grew up in her care and developed into a fine young man.

Time passed, and the grandmother's health began to get worse. She couldn't live at home without a full-time nurse and helper. After discussing the situation with Daniel, the grandmother decided to move to a nursing home, where she would be taken care of.

As the date for his grandmother's move to the nursing home approached, Daniel helped to pack her items and clothing. "I also want to take the piano with me," she said. In the corner of the living room stood the impressive grand piano, on top of which there were photos of Daniel's parents. Daniel knew that his grandmother was a top-notch pianist. That is, until the accident. Since that terrible day, she had not even lifted up the lid of the piano.

"You want to take the piano with you?" said Daniel in surprise. "But you don't use it, Grandma!"

"Of course I use it," she said.

Daniel wanted to say that using the piano for putting pictures on is not considered "using it," but he decided to keep quiet. If it was so important to his beloved grandmother to move the piano to the nursing home, then he would do it. At least it would make it easier for her to get used to her new surroundings.

A few months after Daniel's grandmother moved to the nursing home, she became so weak that she could hardly get out of bed. At that time, Daniel met a young woman and they decided to get married.

Daniel's grandmother managed to come to his wedding but passed away a few weeks later. One day, Daniel's wife opened the piano and tried to play but all she heard was a faint, low sound. She opened the lid of the piano and looked inside. Then she let out a cry of surprise. "Daniel, come look!"

Daniel hurried over and peeked inside. The piano was filled with numerous small, neatly folded notes from old notebooks, slips of paper, brown wrapping paper, receipts, accounts, and anything that could be used to write on.

"What's all this?" asked Daniel in surprise. He stuck his hand in and took out one of the notes. He immediately recognized his grandmother's shaky handwriting. It said: "Thank You Hashem for the miracle that You did for me—Daniel married such an amazing young lady."

He reached in, pulled out another note and read it: "Thank You Hashem for the small miracle that you did for me—I asked Daniel to come over and visit, and he came."

Daniel, who was very moved by this, began to take out the piles of notes. Every now and again, he opened and read another note: "Hashem, thank You for the small miracle that you did for me. I thought that the fridge was broken. I prayed that it wouldn't be true and now everything's okay."

"Hashem, thank You for the wonderful child who helped me schlep the heavy grocery bags home."

"Hashem, thank You for making sure that the cake I made for the guests was such a big hit."

"Hashem, thank You for giving me the money to pay the electricity bill."

The hours flew by. Daniel and his wife became very emotional. They kept on reading the thank-you letters that his grandmother had written throughout the years. Anything good that happened to her was considered a miracle. Even when things were bad, she always found something positive about them.

By now, the carpet was filled with piles of notes, and the piano was almost completely empty. Daniel reached down to the bottom of the piano and pulled out the last note, on which was written: "Hashem, You took away my husband, my son, and my daughter-in-law, but You let me keep my grandson, Daniel. I am so grateful to You for this miracle. Now I have a reason to live."

CHALLENGE FOR THE WEEK

This week, let's try to thank Hashem every day for all the good things that He does for us—even for the things that don't seem so important to us.

How to Say a Berachah Properly

Shimon was starving. It wasn't suppertime yet, and it was too late to wash for bread and sit down for a meal. But what could he eat right now?

"What's there to eat?" he asked Imma.

"Open the fridge," suggested Imma. "There are lots of fruits and vegetables. Help yourself."

Shimon opened the fridge. Peppers? No. Cucumbers? No. He wasn't in the mood right now for washing, cutting, and peeling. Maybe he would eat a few vegetables at supper. But what else was there to eat right now?

Oh, there were apples. Apples are a great snack because you just have to wash them and they're ready to eat, he thought. Shimon chose an apple from the basket, rinsed it, mumbled something, and took a bite.

"Wait a second!" his mother interrupted. "What about a berachah?"

"I said a berachah!" said Shimon firmly, and quickly swallowed the piece.

"That's how a person makes a berachah?" wondered Imma in surprise.

"Yes, I made a berachah. I remember that I said a berachah! I said every word of the berachah!" he insisted.

"Interesting," responded Imma, "It looked as if you were talking to the apple. I saw you whispering something to it."

Shimon felt a little embarrassed. He looked at the half-eaten apple in his hand and remembered that he had mumbled something quickly over it, a minute ago. Really, that's how he said the berachah? Is this the way to thank Hashem for all the healthy and tasty food He gives? Is this how to ask permission from Hashem to eat whatever He has so kindly given him?

How embarrassing!

QUESTIONS FOR THE FAMILY

- How do you make a *berachah*? Slowly and carefully, or in a rush?
- How long should it take to make a *berachah*?

In this week's *parashah*, it says: "And Yosef said to his brothers, 'Please come closer to me,' and they came. And he said, 'I am Yosef, your brother who you sold to Egypt'" (*Bereishis* 45:4).

The Midrash (*Bereishis Rabbah* 93:10) mentions that because of this event, Abba Kohen Bardalah would say, "May Hashem save us from the Day of Judgment! May Hashem save us from the Day of Rebuke!" The Midrash adds that Yosef was the gentlest of the tribes and they *still* weren't able to handle his rebuke, as it says, "And his brothers

were not able to answer him because they were shocked by him." When Hashem will come and rebuke each person individually, as it says: "I will rebuke you and lay it out clearly before you" (*Tehillim* 50:21), how much more so…

Many early commentaries ask the following question on this Midrash: Where is there any rebuke in the *pesukim*? All that Yosef said to his brothers was, "I am Yosef, is my father still alive?" (*Bereishis* 45:3). Where is the rebuke here?

This question was addressed by the Beis HaLevi, the great Rabbi Yosef Dov HaLevi Soloveitchik, *zt"l*. The Beis HaLevi asks: Why did Yosef ask his brothers, "Is my father still alive?" Yehudah had constantly talked about the pain that would be caused to Yaakov if Binyamin would be imprisoned. So what was the question? Obviously, Yaakov was alive!

The Beis HaLevi answered that the best type of rebuke is the rebuke where the wrongdoer realizes, on his own, that he made a mistake. This is similar to the rebuke about the "poor person's lamb." When Nasan HaNavi wanted to rebuke Dovid HaMelech about what happened with Batsheva, he told him that a wealthy person once stole and killed a poor person's lamb. Dovid was very upset and said, "I swear by Hashem's name that the person who did this should be killed!" At that exact moment, Nasan HaNavi said to him, "*You* are that man."

This is exactly how Yosef rebuked his brothers. His (so-called unnecessary) question—if his father was still alive—was actually the rebuke. When Yehudah tried to argue that Yosef would cause a lot of pain and suffering to Yaakov, Yosef asked him, "Is my father still alive?" This means that Yosef was really telling him, "Right now, you're accusing me of making Yaakov feel bad. Why weren't you worried about him suffering twenty-two years ago when you sold me to the Egyptians?!"

This is what Hashem is going to do in the future. When a person will try to make excuses, Hashem will show him how he contradicted himself by what he *himself* said.

For example, a person will eventually be asked in Heaven why he didn't learn Torah. Some will say, "I didn't have time."

"You didn't have time?" they'll ask, and then they'll show him that he had time to read the newspaper.

They'll ask him: "Why didn't you make a *berachah* before you ate?" And if he says that he did, then they'll show him the way that he made a *berachah*. For example, instead of saying, *"borei pri ha'eitz,"* he said, *"bocht'feitz."*

"We don't understand what you said," they'll say to him. "You said a *berachah* that we've never heard of."

There was once a wedding that took place in the city of Ramla, Israel. The *kallah*'s father had money in his suit jacket to pay the hall owner at the end of the wedding.

Sometime during the wedding, the *kallah*'s father took off his jacket, put it on a chair, and danced the *mitzvah tantz* with the *kallah*. At the end of the night, when he went to take the money out of his suit jacket and pay the owner of the hall, he discovered that the money was gone. He was so upset but there was nothing to do.

The next day, the two families got together to celebrate *sheva berachos*. During the meal, they watched the wedding video. During one scene, the video camera suddenly zoomed in on the *kallah*'s father, who took off his jacket and put it on the chair. Everyone strained their eyes, hoping that the cameraman had also focused on the thief himself.

Sure enough, they then saw a person walk up to the jacket, take out the money, and put it in his own pocket. They later discovered that it was actually the *chassan*'s father!

The *chassan*'s father, who was also there watching at the time, fainted on the spot.

The time will come when everybody will find out the truth. Hopefully, we'll never have to suffer the terrible embarrassment that comes from doing the wrong thing.

CHALLENGE FOR THE WEEK

This week, let's try to say all our *berachos* slowly and with *kavanah*.

The Value of a Smile

Shimon opened his eyes in surprise and asked, "Who woke me up?" He blinked from the bright light and said, "Oh, it's from the window." His younger brother had woken up early that morning and decided to wake everyone up in a creative way. He had lifted up the screen all the way. Rays of sunshine now streamed onto Shimon's face and stopped him from sleeping anymore, so he got up, washed his hands, said Modeh Ani, and looked at the clock. "Wow, it's so early!" he said, surprised. He still had another full hour to sleep.

Shimon turned over to the other side, closed his eyes, and tried to fall asleep. But the beams of light were shining all over the room even when his eyes were completely closed. He jumped out of bed angrily and slammed the screen down. "Aaaaargh!"

He climbed back into bed but didn't manage to fall asleep, no matter how much he tried.

Realizing that it was hopeless, he got out of bed and began to get dressed. It was so annoying! He had lost a whole hour

of sleep and now he would be tired the whole day! When his younger brother walked into the room at that moment, Shimon glared at him and grumbled, "Why did you wake me?"

His brother turned around and ran out. It wasn't fun to be around someone who was bitter and angry. Shimon carried on complaining to himself. Huh, it's so frustrating! I could've slept another hour. He woke me up for nothing!

He went into the kitchen to make himself a cup of chocolate milk. Imma greeted him with a warm smile but Shimon just grumbled a "Good morning." It sounded almost as if he said, "What a bad morning."

"What happened to you, Shimon?" wondered Imma.

"He woke me up for nothing!" he exclaimed. "For no reason. He just came and opened the screen, and then the sun was shining right in my face!"

"That's really terrible," agreed Imma. "But you're already up, right?" You actually got something good out of it because now you're ready an hour earlier. Now you have time to eat without rushing. You can also sit and schmooze with me in peace and quiet, without anyone disturbing us. Why not enjoy the next couple of minutes?"

Enjoy?! Could he really change his mood just like that?

QUESTIONS FOR THE FAMILY

- Do you usually smile a lot?
- When you wake up, are you friendly to everyone at home?

Among other *berachos*, Yaakov Avinu blessed Yehudah that he would have so much that he would have "red eyes from wine and white teeth from milk" (*Bereishis* 49:12).

It says in *Maseches Kesubos* (111b): "It's better to give a bright, white smile to a friend than to give milk to him."

A smile is the best thing that you can give to someone else. Rav Shlomo Zalman Auerbach, *zt"l*, explains this idea with the following example:

> *Imagine that it's Shavuos night at the Kotel. Everyone stays awake the entire night, learning and davening vasikin. In the morning, they are about to start heading home, exhausted. The walk back will take a while. At the Kotel exit, somebody has donated huge containers of milk from which everyone can help themselves—free of charge. Can you imagine the impression that this incredible chessed would make? Everyone in Yerushalayim would talk about it and journalists may even interview the donor. Even so, Chazal say that if this donor would stand at the Kotel exit and smile at everyone, this would be worth more than all the glasses of milk that he gave out!"*

The *mishnayos* in *Pirkei Avos* also emphasize how important it is to smile: "Shamai says…Greet every person with a warm, friendly face" (*Avos* 1:15). "Rabbi Yishmael says: Greet every person with joy" (*Avos* 3:12).

It's so important to smile at people because it makes them feel good. When we get home from school, let's walk in with a huge smile on our face. When Abba comes home at night, let's greet him happily. When we smile, we're actually doing many mitzvos. We're making people happy, and we are doing a *chessed* for them.

There was once a prisoner who promised Rabbi Aryeh Levine, *zt"l*, that he would never smoke on Shabbos again. When Rabbi Levine asked him why, he said that the rabbi had come up to him that Shabbos morning, welcomed him with an incredible smile, and patted his hand. The prisoner said, "At that time, I was holding a lit cigarette in my other hand. All I can tell you is that at that exact moment, I felt as if the cigarette was burning my skin. I asked myself, 'How can it be that the rabbi can pat my one hand and make me feel so good while my other hand is holding a lit cigarette on the holy Shabbos?!' On the spot, I promised that I would never ever smoke again on Shabbos."

CHALLENGE FOR THE WEEK

This week, let's try to smile at each family member when we wake up in the morning —and at other times during the day.

Thinking about Others

The bell rang. It was the end of the lesson.

The rebbi closed his Gemara and kissed it. The students also quickly closed their sefarim and ran out of the classroom. There was already a long line by the sinks outside as the boys rushed to wash their hands before sitting down to eat.

The rebbi stood next to the sink and watched the boys wash their hands. Reuven was also watching them. He noticed how Shimon did it too quickly and didn't pour water over the whole hand. Gadi forgot to roll up his long sleeve so he also only washed halfway up his hand. Yehudah didn't dry his hands; he just patted his hands on the towel and returned to his seat. And Moishie said the berachah so quietly that nobody could even answer amen.

Not everybody washed like that. Some boys actually did wash properly. When it was Reuven's turn, he was very careful to keep all the halachos. He poured plenty of water on each hand, twice on the right hand, twice on the left hand. After washing, he shook off the water from his hands, lifted them up, and said the berachah, "Asher kedishanu...al netilas yadayim," and went to dry them on the towel.

Even so, Reuven noticed that the rebbi was not happy about something.

What was the problem? What didn't he do properly? He washed like he should have, said the berachah aloud, didn't push anyone, and didn't disturb any of his friends. So what happened? What did the rebbi want?

Maybe he was just imagining it all? Maybe the rebbi didn't want anything from him.

But he wasn't imagining it. After everyone had already sat down in the classroom and was eating, the rebbi walked in. He stopped and said, "My dear children, do you know that when you go to wash your hands, you have the opportunity to do a very important mitzvah?"

"Sure," yelled several boys at the same time, "the mitzvah of netilas yadayim!"

"That's true," smiled the rebbi, "but that's not what I mean. You can grab another important mitzvah along the way: chessed. You want to know how? Here, I'll tell you..."

QUESTION FOR THE FAMILY

Can you think of how to do *chessed* for other people while doing the mitzvah of *netilas yadayim*?

In the yeshiva of Kfar Chassidim, Rabbi Eliyahu Lopian, the *mashgiach*, made a rule that each person should fill the washing cup for the next person after him. He explained as follows: "We have to train

ourselves to think about others and their needs. That's why it's good for each person to fill the cup for somebody else."

It's a good idea to get into the habit of doing this at home.

In this week's *parashah*, it says about Moshe Rabbeinu:

> "And at that time, Moshe became great and went out to his people, and he saw their suffering" (Shemos 2:11).
>
> Rashi: He focused his eyes and his heart [on them] so that he would feel sorry for them.

At the time of the slavery in Egypt, Moshe Rabbeinu was in the royal palace. Moshe obviously heard about the slavery and knew that the Jewish People were suffering terrible hardship. Although he himself was safe and comfortable, he didn't ignore them. Instead, "he focused his eyes and his heart so that he would feel sorry for them." He also tried to help them as much as he could and showed them that he cared.

The Midrash describes how Moshe cried for them and begged Hashem to help them. It also says that Moshe asked his fellow Jews to give him a rock so that he could carry it on his shoulders and thereby feel their suffering.

Moshe Rabbeinu showed us how to truly care for other people.

There was an elderly lady in olden-day Yerushalayim who decided to do a mitzvah that nobody else wanted to do. She walked around the streets wearing an apron that had two pockets. The right-hand pocket was for keeping all the pages of Torah and *sheimos* that she found lying on the ground, and in the left-hand pocket, she put every peel, piece of glass, or any other thing that could hurt somebody. This kind lady lived a very long life.

Before she passed away, she went to the *beis din* in the *churvah* of Rabbi Yehudah HaChassid, zt"l, and asked them to write down her final request. She requested that after she passes away, the *chevrah kadishah* should use the apron as the *tachrichim* for her body. When she died, many of the people in Yerushalayim went to her funeral and honored her. The *av beis din* eulogized her and read out her final request.

Three days later, she appeared in a dream to the *av beis din* and told him that they had weighed her good deeds in the Heavenly Court. And when they put the apron pockets on the golden scales, it was specifically the left-hand pocket that made all the difference. The pocket that she had used to do *chessed*—by caring about others and picking up dangerous objects—had tipped the scales toward good in the World to Come!

CHALLENGE FOR THE WEEK

Let's remember to fill up the washing cup for the person who is going to wash after us. Practice this at home (especially on Shabbos) and at school.

Being Grateful to Nonliving Objects

Reuven had already taken off his coat in the stairwell. He didn't need it because it was really warm that day. He raced up the steps two at a time and walked into the house, with the coat dragging behind him. "Hi! Imma, please take down the box of Lego!" he said excitedly.

He left his coat and lunch bag on the floor and ran to his brother and sister, who were already by the huge box. Every couple of months, his mother would take down the small pieces of Lego from the top cupboard and it was so much fun. The baby would stay in the stroller or playpen for the whole afternoon so that he wouldn't swallow a tiny block by mistake. The other children would have a great time connecting the pieces together and would build incredible works of art from the small Lego pieces.

All of a sudden, he heard his mother's voice from the corridor: "What's this? Who threw their coat on the floor?"

Reuven got up immediately, embarrassed. "Sorry, I'll tidy it all up right now," he apologized. He picked up the coat and the bag and hung each one in its place. He certainly didn't want his mother to have to bend down and pick up his items instead of him.

"Apology accepted," said his mother with a smile, "but it's not about me. What about being grateful to the coat that kept you warm and protected you from the rain? And to the schoolbag that saved your food from getting damaged?"

QUESTIONS FOR THE FAMILY

- Why does gratitude apply to nonliving objects too? After all, they don't even have feelings!
- How do you treat your things—with respect or neglect? Can you give an example?

The obligation to be grateful is so important that we are commanded to be grateful to *all* of Hashem's messengers that help us—even to nonliving things.

In this week's *parashah*, we see an example of being grateful to non-living objects: the river and the dust. Chazal ask: Why did Aharon, not Moshe, hit the water? This is because Hashem said to Moshe, "It's not right that the water that protected you when you were thrown into the river should be hit by you. Only Aharon should hit it."

This idea is also mentioned by the plague of frogs. Chazal also said this by the plague of lice. Hashem said to Moshe, "It's not right that the dust, which protected you when you killed the Egyptian, should be hit by you." That's why these three plagues were done by Aharon (*Midrash Rabbah Shemos* 9).

Why is it important to be grateful to something that isn't even alive? After all, everybody knows that the nonliving object didn't *intend* to give us benefit. Also, it won't know that you're grateful either!

Rabbi Eliyahu Eliezer Dessler, zt"l, in his *sefer Michtav Mei'Eliyahu* (volume 3, p. 100), explains that even though the nonliving object itself didn't choose to help the person, nevertheless *we* need to be grateful. We have to express our feelings of gratitude and try to have this attitude toward anything that gives us benefit. If we're not grateful, and treat the object with disrespect, then we'll eventually deny the good that Hashem gives us.

How do we show our gratitude to something that's not living? By not causing damage to something that we used, i.e., not breaking or neglecting it, and by positive actions that help the object (for example, keeping the shul clean).

Another example of showing gratitude to that which is nonliving is regarding food. Chazal say that "one should not walk past food that's lying on the ground." This means that if someone sees food lying on the ground in a disrespectful way, he should pick it up because a person has to be grateful to food because it keeps him alive. Although that specific food didn't give him any benefit, it is still from the general category of food from which the person benefits.

Here are a few short stories about being grateful to objects:

> *One morning after Shacharis, Rabbi Eliyahu Lopian was holding his tallis while walking and talking with a student. When he walked past a nearby bench, he put his tallis on the bench and folded it. But then Rabbi Lopian noticed that the bench was dirty. He went to get a towel to clean the bench. The student rushed to get the towel so that Rabbi Lopian wouldn't have to trouble himself. Rabbi Lopian stopped him and said, "Please let me—I am grateful to the bench on which I folded my tallis."*
>
> *When the Klausenberger Rebbe, zt"l, would walk into the lobby of the yeshiva and notice the piles of sefarim that had piled*

up on the tables, he would remind the students to treat the sefarim with more respect. He would end off with the following words: "Aside from the actual obligation to treat sacred books with respect, a person also has to be grateful to the sefer and its author. That's because he was able to benefit from this sefer. So why shouldn't he treat it with a sense of gratitude and put it back in its right place on the bookshelf?"

People say that the Rosh Yeshiva of Netzach Yisrael, Rabbi Yisrael Ze'ev Gustman, zt"l, would personally water the bushes that were in the garden of the yeshiva. He did this because when he ran away from Vilna due to the Nazis, he dived under one of the bushes to hide from those who were chasing him. This is how he was saved from being killed. As a result, he was forever grateful to the bushes, and would water them personally as a sign of this gratitude. Although the bushes in the yeshiva's garden weren't the same bushes that saved him, nevertheless, they were similar to the ones that saved him and he was grateful to those bushes too.

CHALLENGE FOR THE WEEK

When we come home, let's try to put our bags, sweaters, or coats where they belong. This shows our appreciation for our things.

Doing Things Right Away

"Good morning!"

Reuven's mother walked into the bedroom and pulled open the curtains. Bright rays of sun shone into the room as she announced, "Reuven, it's time to get up."

Reuven simply turned over and went back to sleep.

His mother sighed, walked up to him, and gently patted him on the shoulder. "Reuven, good morning!"

"Good morning," groaned Reuven and lifted the blanket over his ears.

"Great!" said his mother excitedly. "You're up." She turned around and left the room. She had a lot to do in the morning and didn't have time to hang around.

Reuven continued sleeping. In the rest of the house, there was a lot of action. His brothers and sisters got up, dressed, drank their milk, and got their food ready for the rest of the day. But Reuven carried on dozing away peacefully.

A half hour later, Reuven's mother walked into the room again.

She stood in shock as she noticed the blanket gently rising and falling in rhythm with the boy's breathing. "What's going on? Reuven, it's so late!" She pulled the blanket away and yelled, "Get up already, Reuven!"

But Reuven just pulled the blanket over himself again and mumbled, "Soon."

"Soon?" said his mother anxiously. "If you don't get up right now, you're going to be late."

Eventually, Reuven opened his eyes. He dragged himself over to the washing cup and slowly washed his hands. He began to dress at a snail's pace. The bed seemed to be calling him back. All he wanted was to get back into bed, cover himself with the blanket, and go back to sleep. That's exactly what he would have done—if his mother wasn't standing next to him.

But his mother knew her beloved child too well. Even though they were calling her from the kitchen and it was getting very late, she stood next to Reuven and helped him to get ready.

"Now the pants...Wait, put the sleeping kippah in its place...The shoes are here, under the chair...Close the buttons properly..." And every now and again: "Nu, faster!" and "Reuven, hurry—it's late already!"

As expected, he didn't manage to drink his milk, but at least he left the house on time. His mother waved goodbye to him and as she watched him moving further away, she sighed to herself. What will be, my child? How long will the mornings continue to be like a marathon where the runner doesn't cooperate at all?

QUESTIONS FOR THE FAMILY

- Do you get up quickly every morning?
- Sometimes it's difficult to get up. How can we beat that feeling of laziness and jump out of bed on time?

It says in this week's *parashah*, "And you should guard the matzos" (*Shemos* 12:17).

Rashi brings the following quote from the *Mechilta*: "Rabbi Yoshiya says: 'Don't read it as the 'matzos,' but rather as the 'mitzvos.' Just as we don't let the matzos get spoiled, so too we shouldn't let the mitzvos become 'spoiled.' If you're able to do a mitzvah, then do it immediately."

We learn from this how important it is to do mitzvos right away.

People say that Rabbi Eliezer Menachem Shach, *zt"l*, would jump out of bed, even when he was very old. When they asked him why, he told them that if he didn't get up right away, then he wouldn't get up at all. This is because the *yetzer hara* would already have convinced him not to get up.

One morning before *Shacharis*, the *mashgiach* Rabbi Nosson Wachtfogel, *zt"l*, said that he had just seen two people who had unfortunately been kidnapped. He said that he had tried to help them but didn't manage. He was very sad about it. The people who heard him talk about it wondered where the *mashgiach* had been that morning. How could he have met these people before *Shacharis*? That's when the *mashgiach* explained that he had seen two *bachurim* who didn't get up on time for *davening*, and were "trapped in jail by the old foolish king" (i.e., the *yetzer hara*) who caught them in his trap.

It is told regarding the great gaon Rabbi Boruch Ber Leibovitz, *zt"l*, author of the *Birkas Shmuel*, that he would imagine that the *Sha'agas Aryeh* and the *Nesivos* were standing next to him when he woke up, and that they were waiting eagerly for him to wash his hands so that he could learn their Torah thoughts.

An *avreich* once walked into a shul on Chol Hamoed and was asked to give a short, inspiring talk to the people. He agreed and this is what he said: "When the Jewish People left Egypt and arrived at the Yam Suf, they were very scared. Thousands of Jewish men, women, and children were standing there with the raging sea in front of them. The Egyptians were behind and about to catch up to them. At that moment, they needed an act of self-sacrifice to save them. Among everyone, there was a person whose name was *Gershon* ben Aminadav."

The congregation was surprised by his mistake and immediately corrected him. "It was *Nachshon* ben Aminadav, not *Gershon!*" they shouted.

But the speaker pretended as if he didn't hear, and continued.

"Gershon didn't know what to do. On the one hand, somebody had to jump into the water and give up his life. On the other hand, what would happen to his wife and young children? Who would take care of them after he drowned? In the end, Gershon ben Aminadav decided that he would give up his life."

Meanwhile, somebody went up to the *gabbai* and complained to him, "This person doesn't know anything! Why did you ask him to speak?"

The speaker continued talking: "Eventually, *Gershon* ben Aminadav decided to jump in. But to his great surprise, who did he meet there? *Nachshon* ben Aminadav, who had jumped in a few moments before. If Nachshon hadn't beaten Gershon to it, then Gershon would've gotten credit for the miracle. But he waited and so he lost out on the incredible *zechus* of doing such a massive *kiddush Hashem*. When a person has a certain idea, he should do it right away—before somebody else does it."

CHALLENGE FOR THE WEEK

Let's try to get up every morning right away.

PARASHAS BESHALACH

Being Grateful
to Animals

Reuven came home, walked into the kitchen, and smelled lots of yummy things cooking. He lifted the lids of the pots, peeked inside, and asked his mother, "When's lunch?"

Surprised, his mother asked, "What happened today? Usually, you say that you aren't hungry. And then we have to call you so many times until you decide to come and eat. Didn't you eat your bread at school today?"

Reuven looked down. "No, I didn't eat it," he said quietly.

His mother opened his lunch bag. "Hey, where's your sandwich? It's not here."

"It's not in the bag," admitted Reuven. "I put it on the ledge outside the window of the classroom."

"Why?" said his mother, somewhat curious and a little upset. She had worked hard to make Reuven's sandwich that morning. She had fried an egg, cut two slices of bread—not too thick and not too thin (exactly as her fussy son liked)—put the egg

between them, and added slices of tomato and cucumber. And after all that, her son had decided to put it outside on the ledge, instead of eating it?!

"It was for the birds," explained Reuven, sounding a little sorry.

"For the birds?!" exclaimed his mother. "But today isn't Shabbos Shirah!"

"You're right," the boy agreed. "But who said that the birds should only get to eat on Shabbos Shirah? Why should they be hungry the whole year?"

"And why should **you** be hungry?" asked his mother in the same tone. "Why give bread with egg and vegetables to the poor birds? Who says that they like that type of sandwich? Maybe they tasted it and said, 'Oy, what a pity! We thought that it was a nice dry, tasty piece of bread but it turned out to be all soggy and oily; that's not what we wanted.' And I spent so much time making it!"

Reuven smiled but his mother was quite serious. "Look, Reuven. It's true that the birds helped Am Yisrael when they were in the desert. And that's why we feed them—to show our appreciation. But it doesn't say that you should give them the school lunch that I made for you! Let's make a deal that whenever we have dry bread left over, I'll give it to you. Then you can take it and put it in a place where the birds can get it. But you must eat the sandwich that I make for you for school—no matter what, okay?"

Reuven agreed. His mother smiled, took the lids off the pots, and filled up her son's plate with lots of yummy food.

QUESTIONS FOR THE FAMILY

- Why is it important to be grateful to animals?
- Can you think of other animals that helped us a long time ago that we still show appreciation to?

Many people have a *minhag* to put out crumbs of bread for birds on *Shabbos Shirah* (*Orach Chaim* 324: *Mishnah Berurah* 31). This is because of the following story that took place after the Jews came out of Egypt. Two wicked people, Dasan and Aviram, took *mann* and spread it all over the camp on Friday night. They did this to disprove Moshe Rabbeinu's announcement that "there would not be *mann* on Shabbos" (*Shemos* 16:26). They went and told the people that they should go outside and see that there was *mann* on the ground. Even though some people went out to look, they didn't manage to find any *mann*—because the birds had already eaten it all! The breadcrumbs we leave out on *Shabbos Shirah* are a reward for birds because they ate the *mann* in the desert (*Ta'amei HaMinhagim* in the name of HaRav HaTzaddik from Lublin).

Here are some more examples of showing gratitude to living creatures:

There is a mitzvah to redeem a donkey. When a firstborn donkey is born, a person must redeem it. It does have some degree of *kedushah*, but since it is *tamei* and cannot be brought as a *korban*, it must be redeemed with a sheep. Why did only the donkey deserve to get this mitzvah?

We find the answer in *Bechoros* 5b: "Why are firstborn donkeys different from firstborn horses and camels? Because they helped the Jews when they left Egypt. Every single Jew had ninety Libyan donkeys, loaded with gold and silver from Egypt."

The dog is also rewarded for not barking when the Jews left Egypt. The *pasuk* says: "And you may not eat the meat of an animal that was attacked in the field; you should throw it to the dog" (*Shemos* 22:30). Rashi explains that Hashem always rewards an animal if it deserves it. The Torah says: "And the dog did not bark at any of the Jewish People," so Hashem said: "Give the dog its reward."

Chazal in *Talmud Yerushalmi* (*Terumos* 44b) tell a story about a person who would invite *gedolei olam* to his home and let his dog sit next to them. People asked him why he did that, because it seemed so disrespectful to them! He told them that an incredible miracle had happened to him because of the dog. One day, a group of dangerous people attacked his wife and tried to kidnap her. The dog bit them and they ran away, and his wife was saved; he wanted to show his appreciation to the dog, and the *rabbanim* agreed.

There is another miracle that happened with an animal in a certain *yishuv* in Israel. One day, a donkey appeared and started walking toward the gate of the *yishuv*. As it got closer, one of the guard dogs jumped up and attacked it. When the donkey fell down, some of the local people ran over and discovered that it was strapped with several bombs. If it had *chas v'shalom* exploded in the *yishuv*, there would have probably been a terrible tragedy. When the people from the *yishuv* discussed this incident with Rav Yitzchak Zilberstein, *shlita*, he told them to find the dog that had bitten the donkey and give it the donkey's body out of appreciation.

CHALLENGE FOR THE WEEK

Let's put out some bread crumbs for the birds one day this week (to show that we also think of them during the week and not just on *Shabbos Shirah*).

Honoring Parents

"Reuven, did you finish eating supper?"

Reuven looked up from the puzzle he had been working on for the last half hour. "A long time ago," he answered, quite surprised.

"Then why are your supper things still on the table?" his mother asked.

He stood up and peeked into the kitchen. Oy, the table sure was a mess. There was a plate with some leftover salad, a fork that still had a little egg on it, an empty yogurt container with a used spoon, a cup with some leftover chocolate milk, and a piece of dry bread—all of which he had completely forgotten about.

"Oh, that," said Reuven as he kneeled down again next to the puzzle. "Okay, I'll clean it up soon."

Fifteen minutes went by. Reuven was making progress on the puzzle and had completely forgotten about his mother's request.

"Reuven," his mother reminded him, "your supper things are still waiting to be cleaned up."

"Okay, no problem," Reuven shouted from his room. "I'm coming in a little while."

"In a little while?!" shouted back his mother. She didn't want to wait any longer. She threw the empty yogurt container and dry piece of bread into the garbage, and put the dirty utensils in the sink. Enough was enough!

It was getting late. Reuven finished making the puzzle, broke it up and left the pieces where they were. He went to draw pictures of lions, like his friend Dovid had taught him. First, he drew a heart, and then a bigger heart around it, added the eyes, then a triangle for the nose, a circle for the mouth, a huge mane, and finally two ears. And there it was—a really neat picture of a lion.

He used up quite a few pages while practicing drawing his impressive-looking lions. He crumpled up whatever didn't turn out well and threw it on the floor. That's when his mother walked into the room and got a fright. "What a mess! Reuven, please tidy up whatever you left lying around! It's late already. You need to go to sleep."

Reuven looked at the clock—it really was late. He climbed onto his bed and lay down. He hadn't realized how tired he was until now.

"Reuven," his mother said. "This is not the time to lie down. You need to tidy up the room now and go shower, then you can sleep."

"I can't clean it all up now!" said Reuven with a yawn, as he looked at the floor. About a hundred puzzle pieces, quite a few scraps of paper, a bunch of markers and pencils, and a lot of pencil shavings. He sure didn't feel like doing all that work right now.

"So who's going to clean your room?" his mother asked.

And that's exactly the question. Who would do it?

QUESTIONS FOR THE FAMILY

- Does this also sometimes happen to you?
- What should we do?

Everybody wants to honor Hashem. If Hashem would come to us and personally ask us to do something, we would definitely run to do it.

But there's another way for a person to honor Hashem.

In this week's *parashah* (*Shemos* 20:12), it says: "Honor your father and your mother."

The Gemara (*Kiddushin* 30b) says that if a person honors his parents, Hashem considers it as if the person honored Him. So if we do what our parents want as soon as they ask, then it's as if we did exactly what Hashem wanted.

Here are other examples about the connection between honoring parents and honoring Hashem:

1. The Gemara (*Kiddushin* 31b) says that when Rabbi Yosef heard the sound of his mother walking, he stood up quickly to honor his mother and said, "I'm now going to stand up for the *Shechinah*, which is arriving."

2. On the *Luchos*, the mitzvos "between a person and Hashem" are on the right side, while the mitzvos "between a person and his friend" are on the left side. If so, why is the mitzvah to honor parents on the *right* side? The answer is that this shows that there is a connection between honoring Hashem and honoring parents.

The Gerrer Rebbe, Rabbi Avraham Mordechai Alter, zt"l, was once traveling on a train from Warsaw to Biala, where his father-in-law lived. For almost the entire time, he sat with his Gemara and learned. A fellow Jew sat down on the seat opposite him and watched him the whole time. He was amazed that the Rebbe kept on learning, nonstop.

But all of a sudden, in the middle of the night, the Rebbe took out his watch and exclaimed, "Oy, it's almost midnight!" He quickly closed the Gemara, opened his suitcase, and took out some sandwiches. He washed his hands and ate everything as if he was in a rush.

When the Rebbe saw that the other Jew was so surprised by this, he turned to him and explained: "I really wasn't hungry, but my mother gave me this food and told me that I had to finish all of it today. So that's why I ate in such a rush."

CHALLENGE FOR THE WEEK

If Imma or Abba ask us to do something, let's try to do it right away. Imagine that Hashem asked us to do it.

Not Telling a Lie

Reuven was sitting at the kitchen table, trying to teach a cute game to his brother and sister. It was about tapping with one's fingers on the table, in a specific order. Index finger, middle finger, fourth finger…index finger, middle finger, fourth finger. Or index finger, pinky…index finger, pinky. He also did it with all the fingers together: index finger, middle finger, fourth finger, pinky, and then did it again.

"Be careful!" his sister shouted. "There's a glass plate here."

Reuven didn't seem to care about the warning. The plate was on the other side of the table and didn't look like it was on the edge. What was all the fuss about?

He continued tapping to the rhythm: index finger, fourth finger, middle finger, pinky… "Wow, this is difficult! Again." Index finger, fourth finger, middle finger —

Craaaaash!

The plate fell on the floor and shattered into thousands of pieces.

"What did you do?" his brother gasped.

"Why didn't you watch out?' his sister asked angrily.

Reuven looked in shock at all the pieces of glass that were all over the kitchen floor. "Oy vey! How'd they even get into all those places?!"

When his mother heard the noise, she ran to the kitchen. "What happened?" she asked and stood still, looking at all the tiny pieces of glass. "What's this? Was it a plate?"

The children nodded their heads and their mother bent down to look at the floor.

"Oy, when these plates break, it's a major problem. There are pieces all over the place!" she moaned. "Wait, kids. Don't get off the chairs! Don't walk on the floor! I need to pick up all the pieces of glass around here. Nobody is allowed to come into the kitchen barefoot for the whole afternoon."

She picked up the baby and carefully took him out of the kitchen. Then she came back, lifted up Reuven's little sister, and also carried her to a different room.

She didn't take Reuven out. He was too heavy and was also old enough to know how to sit quietly without disturbing while she cleaned the floor.

Reuven sat quietly on the chair, picked up his feet so that he wouldn't disturb his mother, and looked miserably at the shiny glass fragments. "Gosh, now the baby won't be able to crawl here. Even after a thorough cleaning and scrubbing, there will probably still be some sharp pieces around," he thought.

Reuven's mother went out of the kitchen and returned a minute later with a broom and dustpan. She began to sweep up the numerous fragments and groaned again. "Who did this?" she asked suddenly, and looked at Reuven. "Was it you?"

Reuven didn't know what to answer. If he admitted that he was the careless one who had caused this whole headache, his mother would probably punish him. But if he said that it wasn't him, then it would be a lie!

QUESTIONS FOR THE FAMILY

- What do you think Reuven should do?
- Where does it say that you're not allowed to lie?

It says in the *parashah*: "מדבר שקר תרחק—Stay far away from a lie" (*Shemos* 23:7). The Torah doesn't use the words "stay away" with any other *aveirah*. This shows us how terrible it is to tell a lie.

The Gemara (*Sanhedrin* 92a) says that Rabbi Eliezer said, "Anyone who tells a lie it is as if he worshipped idols." Let's think about this. If someone threatened a person that he must convert to Christianity or else be killed, he would certainly refuse. After all, idol worship is listed as one of the three severe sins about which it says, "Be killed and don't transgress." And now Rabbi Eliezer is telling us that if a person lies, it is considered as bad as if he worships idols! We see from here that it is so important to improve ourselves in this area and not tell lies.

The following story was featured in a book by Menucha Beckerman.

A class of schoolchildren wanted to have a siyum to celebrate that they finished learning the Chumash. The celebration was scheduled for a certain date. The rebbi announced that every-one had to do their homework and whoever didn't do it would not be able to join the siyum party.

Menachem was about to do the homework but then Aunt Bella and her three young children arrived. He played with them and completely forgot about the homework. And he only remem-bered when the class started to set up the next day.

"Oy vey! I completely forgot about the homework," he said to himself. Menachem was worried and cried out, "What now? There's no time for me to do it now."

"I also didn't do the work," whispered Mordechai. A few more boys said that they didn't do the work. But they said that they weren't going to tell the rebbi and that he would forget about it anyway. Even so, Menachem refused to do that. He kept thinking to himself: *The rebbi definitely said that whoever didn't do the homework wouldn't be allowed to come to the siyum party. If I stay, he'll think I did the work—and I don't want to be a liar.*

He left the classroom, sat down somewhere, and began to do the work.

When the rebbi came in to the class, he noticed that Menachem's seat was empty.

"Where is Menachem?" asked the rebbi. They replied that he was sitting outside in the corridor.

The rebbi walked outside and found Menachem crying. "What's wrong, Menachem? Why aren't you in class?" he asked.

Menachem looked up and said, "I forgot to do the work yesterday because some family came over to visit. And you said that whoever doesn't do the work wouldn't be at the siyum."

"But I didn't even know that you didn't do the work!" said the rebbi, quite amazed.

"That's true but I still didn't want to pretend as if I did it. I knew that I didn't do the work and I didn't want the rebbi to think that I had done the work."

The rebbi took the boy into class and said, "Look, everybody. Menachem is becoming a real ben Torah—a boy who the Torah is really proud of. He told the truth. Even though nobody knew that he didn't do the work, he still decided to tell the truth. This is the way to grow in Torah. Someone who is honest is really special."

Then the rebbi added: "And because Menachem did what the Torah wanted, I am choosing him to be the Chasan Torah at this siyum."

CHALLENGE FOR THE WEEK

Can you give an example of how you or somebody else told the truth?

PARASHAS TERUMAH

Giving Tzedakah

Reuven was the first to hear the knocking. "Somebody's knocking!" he shouted.

His younger brother ran to the door. He always liked to open it and see who was there. Their mother also came. Both of them were surprised to see such a poor-looking man standing there. His clothing was torn, his beard was scruffy, and he looked like he was homeless.

The man stuck out his hand and said: "Tzedakah."

Their mother went over to the shelf in the kitchen where they kept the small change. From where he was sitting on the sofa in the living room, Reuven could see the man. He really looked strange. All of a sudden, his younger brother ran to his desk, grabbed the small wallet that he had gotten as a birthday present, and took out two coins.

"What are you doing?" said Reuven as he got up from the sofa.

"Giving tzedakah!' said his brother proudly. He gave the coins to the man.

The beggar thanked them for the money. "Tizku l'mitzvos!" he said in a croaky voice and walked away.

Reuven went to his brother and asked, "Why did you give him some of your money?"

"Imma lets me," he said, a little annoyed.

"That's not what I meant. I wanted to know why you decided to give him." Reuven explained. His brother didn't understand what the question was. "It's a mitzvah. What's the problem with that?" he said.

Reuven decided to go ask his mother. "Imma, why does a person have to give tzedakah? After all, if Hashem would've wanted this man to have money, wouldn't He have given him? Hashem can give whatever He wants and to whoever He wants. So if Hashem didn't want to give money to the beggar, then why do we need to give to him?"

QUESTIONS FOR THE FAMILY

- Is Reuven right?
- How much money do you have saved up?

If you ask any person, "How much money do you have?" he will probably go count all his money and tell you the total amount. That's not the right answer though. Our true wealth is really only the money that we use to do mitzvos.

In the *parashah*, it says: "And Hashem spoke to Moshe saying, 'And they should *take* a donation for Me'" (*Shemos* 25:2). But when a person donates, doesn't he *give* a donation and not *take* a donation? So why does it say "And they should *take*"?

When a person gives to the *Mishkan* or to a poor person, he is actually taking—for *himself*. This is because the good deed, or *tzedakah*, will help him a lot after he passes away.

This is what the *pasuk* also means when it says, "The poor person is with you." If you give money to a poor person, then this will be your wealth forever and ever.

This is similar to the following riddle. A cat attacked ten birds that were sitting in a row on a roof, and caught two of them. How many birds are left? Most people answer that eight are left. The correct answer though, is that only *two* are left, because the others flew away.

This is the same for tzedakah. The only thing that stays with us is whatever we have given to *tzedakah* and *chessed*. Everything else will not go with us to the next world.

The Gemara (*Bava Basra* 10a) says that the wicked Turnus Rufus asked Rabbi Akiva, "If your G-d loves poor people, why doesn't He take care of them?" Rabbi Akiva told him, "To save *us* from being punished in Gehinnom."

The *Baal Haturim* says an amazing idea about giving. The word "ונתנו" (and he should give) can be read forward (right to left) as well as backward (from left to right). Either way, it always has the same meaning. This shows us that if you give, then it will come back to you, and then you can keep on giving.

There was once a king who told one of his ministers to declare exactly how much money he (the minister) had. When the minister said that he only had a small amount of money, the king got so angry because he knew that the minister was extremely wealthy and owned plenty of property. How dare the minister try to hide most of his wealth from him?! When the king ordered him to come, the minister calmed the king down. He explained as follows: "His royal majesty asked me to present all *my* wealth. And that's exactly what I did. The only money that I have is that which I gave away to charity, and even the king himself cannot take this money away from me. But the rest of what I have is not really mine. That's because if the king wants, he could take it away from me on the spot. My wealth is only the donations and good deeds that I have done."

CHALLENGE FOR THE WEEK

This week, let's try to give *tzedakah* every day. At the end of the week, each person will count how much money he is truly left with.

PARASHAS TETZAVEH

Greeting Parents When Entering the House

Every day Reuven leaves school during the lunch break to eat at home. But one afternoon when he walked into the house, he smelled right away that he wouldn't like the food that day. He couldn't stand fish cutlets in tomato paste! He decided to skip lunch and take some cookies instead.

He went to his room, took the book he had gotten from the library the day before, and lay down on the bed to read. He had over an hour until he had to go back to school. Maybe he would even manage to finish the book. Reuven was so involved in the exciting story, he didn't even notice the tumult that was going on downstairs…

His mother was the first person to start worrying. "Where's Reuven?" she asked and checked the time again. "He was supposed to be home more than fifteen minutes ago."

"Sometimes he takes a little longer, right?" said Reuven's father, not yet worried.

But after a half an hour, he also began to get nervous. Then, when it had been forty-five minutes from the time that Reuven usually came back, they realized that they had to find out where he was.

Reuven's mother phoned Gadi, his friend from class, who lived in the next building. "Are you sure you saw him come back?" She kept on asking, "What? Not a hundred percent sure? It could be that he didn't? Okay, thanks."

She put the phone on the table and looked at her husband nervously. "He's never come back as late as this!"

"Maybe he stayed at school?" wondered her husband aloud.

"Maybe." Reuven's mother felt that her legs were shaking too much and that she couldn't stand. She collapsed on the chair and said weakly, "Call the school to look for him."

"Who would be there now, during the break?" asked Reuven's father, but he dialed anyway.

The secretary answered but didn't know where Reuven was. "If I find out anything, I'll let you know" he said. Reuven's father thanked him. He tried to think of who else could help them find their missing son. Meanwhile, Reuven's mother started saying a perek of Tehillim.

Both of them didn't even notice that the baby had thrown all the food off his plate onto the floor.

His sister did notice, though. She decided to clean up the mess on the floor, so she went to get a rag from the balcony. On the way there, she walked past the boys' room and stopped suddenly at the door. Out of the corner of her eye, she noticed Reuven relaxing on his bed and reading a book. The boy who had "disappeared" and not come home had been there the whole time!

"Reuven!" she shouted. Reuven jumped. He looked up in surprise. "What's the problem?" he asked. When they explained to him the whole story, he couldn't understand why everybody

was so angry with him. What had he done wrong? What was all the fuss about?

QUESTIONS FOR THE FAMILY

- Why is it important to knock on the door before coming in?
- Why is it important to say hello before coming in?

In this week's *parashah*, there are more than forty *pesukim* that talk about the clothes of the *Kohen Gadol*. This is somewhat surprising. Why would the clothing of the *Kohen Gadol* be so interesting?

Sure enough, Chazal learn an important message from every piece of the *Kohen Gadol*'s clothing. Each one helps us to fix something wrong that we did.

Regarding the long robe, the *pasuk* says: "And you shall make pomegranates from turquoise, purple, and scarlet wool on its edges…and gold bells between them all the way around" (*Shemos* 28:33).

What were the golden bells for? The *pasuk* (*Shemos* 28:35) tells us that when the *Kohen Gadol* walked into the *Kodesh* to stand before Hashem, the robe's bells would make a noise.

Why was it important that the bells should make a noise when the *Kohen Gadol* came into the *Kodesh*? Most people would think that he should come into the *Kodesh* gently and quietly, like it says: "Hashem is without a commotion" (*Melachim I* 19:11).

The answer is because the ringing of the bells shows an important idea about the *Kohen Gadol*'s service. Even though Hashem obviously knew he was coming, the *Kohen Gadol* shouldn't walk into the *Kodesh* unexpectedly.

One person told the following story that actually happened in his neighborhood.

I have a neighbor who raises her children with the help of a team of special angels. Otherwise, I don't know how the children would survive. There is only one way to describe how she raises her children—pure negligence. She doesn't watch over her children at all.

One Friday, we got ready to spend Shabbos with my brother who lives in a different city. We hardly ever go away. It wasn't easy to pack up and get everything organized for the trip. On Friday morning, we worked hard to finish up everything quickly. We try not to travel too close to when Shabbos comes in. While the kids took the suitcases down to the car, I did a last-minute check on our home. I made sure that we hadn't forgotten to close all the windows. I also double-checked that the gas pipe was switched off. Everything seemed to be okay, so I walked out and locked the door.

By the time I got to the car, the whole family was already in their seats and ready to go. I buckled myself and we drove off.

We got there in good time and had a great Shabbos. On motzaei Shabbos, we packed up our suitcases again and drove home. As soon as we got back to our parking lot, we just knew that something wasn't right. "Look!" said one of children. "There are cars all over the place here."

"Who's having a simchah?" I asked one of the neighbors who was standing next to the sidewalk.

"Simchah?" She stared at me with a confused look. "You call this terrible situation a simchah?!"

"Terrible situation?" I asked.

"Yes. Benny, the neighbor's baby, has disappeared. He's been missing since Friday."

"Oy vey!" I said. I was about to say something but then I stopped myself. I almost said, "I knew that this would happen. I just didn't know when."

She explained: "Everybody is looking for him. There are search *parties all over the city. Local people are walking all around the neighborhood and the police are on the lookout."*

I walked up the stairs to our home, unlocked the door, and brought the girls in. And there on the floor in a corner, all bundled up, was Benny. I was so shocked that I couldn't move for a minute.

But how did he get there? I thought to myself. I knew I had closed and locked all the windows before we left. The only way he could've gotten there was by sneaking in as we were packing up. If only he had let us know when he came in.

I had to go closer to him to see if he was still alive because he wasn't moving. I was so nervous that my legs were actually shaking. Baruch Hashem, I saw that he was alive. "Oy vey, Hashem! The child hasn't eaten or drunk for more than thirty hours." And he was alone in the dark.

We called an ambulance. When the paramedic checked the boy, he said, "The child is fine. He's very weak, though, and he needs to eat. I'll give him a few drops now and the doctor can decide if he needs an infusion."

Just then, two policemen walked into my home. "How could it be that Benny was locked in your home and you didn't even know about it?" they asked.

At first, I was so angry at them for asking such a question. I felt that they were accusing me of hiding or kidnapping Benny. "Maybe you should ask his mother how it could be," I said. I then told them that I refused to answer any more questions. I was sure that they would take me away to jail, but they didn't. When the police then went and asked a few of the neighbors, they understood what I meant. They realized very quickly that Benny had a habit of roaming all over the place. And that it was a miracle that something like this hadn't happened up until then.

The story of Benny continued. He came home on Monday morning after receiving fluids intravenously. Baruch Hashem,

he seemed to be back to normal. His parents were called in for
an investigation and that's how the incident ended.

Now we know what can happen if someone walks into the house without telling anyone.

CHALLENGE FOR THE WEEK

When we walk into the house this week, let's try to say hello, loud and clear.

Keep on practicing this until it becomes a habit.

Standing Up for Parents

"Hello!" Reuven's father said as he walked into the house. The baby turned around and crawled toward to him, shrieking excitedly, "Abba, Abba!"

Reuven's father smiled at him and said, "Hello, my cutie." He hung his hat on its hook and picked up the baby.

Reuven heard that his father had come home and he called out, "Hello, Abba." He then carried on looking at his comic book. He had already read this comic book five or six times and he knew it almost by heart. But it was a cute story and the pictures were really neat, so he still enjoyed reading it over and over again.

Reuven's father walked into the living room. Reuven's younger brother, who was busy drawing a picture, got up from his chair, holding the paper in his hand. "Abba, look at what I drew."

Reuven's father inspected the drawing and complimented the young artist. "Nice, very nice!" Then he looked at Reuven, who was so busy reading his book that he didn't even notice that his father had walked into the room.

"Hello, Reuven," his father said to him.

Reuven looked up from the book. "Hello," he said for the second time and was about to continue reading.

His father walked up to him, bent down, and said, "Reuven, I'm a little surprised. Usually you remember to do something when I walk in. This time, though, you forgot. Can you guess what it is?"

QUESTIONS FOR THE FAMILY

- Can you guess what Reuven forgot to do?
- Why is it important to stand up when parents walk into the room?

It says in the *parashah*: "And when Moshe went out to the tent, the whole nation stood up" (*Shemos* 33:8).

The *Midrash* (*Tanchuma Parashas Ki Sisa* 27) tells us that this event teaches us that a person should stand up for an elderly person and for a *talmid chacham*. We also learn from the Gemara (*Makkos* 22b) that just as people stand up for a *Sefer Torah*, so should they also stand up for a *talmid chacham*.

Some people would even do unusual things in order to do the mitzvah of getting up to show respect:

> *Rabbi Shalom Schwadron was once waiting at a bris milah. All of a sudden, one of the family members came in and announced that Rav Shach, who was supposed to be the sandek, would be arriving shortly. Rabbi Shalom immediately sat down on the bench in order to honor Rav Shach by standing up when he came in.*

> *The Saba of Slabodka once noticed that the great Rosh Yeshiva Rabbi Moshe Mordechai Epstein was approaching. He*

immediately lay down on the bed nearby. When Rabbi Moshe Mordechai reached him, the Saba got up from the bed and stood upright to give him honor and respect.

One should also stand up for parents out of respect for them, and even more so if they are *talmidei chachamim*.

The following story is mentioned in *Bereishis Rabbasi (Vayishlach)*. One night, Rabbi Yehoshua dreamed about his future place in Gan Eden. In the dream, Eliyahu HaNavi told him: "Be happy because you have the same place and share in Gan Eden as Ninus the butcher, from the village of Kitor."

Rabbi Yehoshua woke up, remembered his dream, and was very upset. "Poor me," he thought. "Since the day I was born, I lived in constant awe of my Creator and put all my efforts into Torah. I never walked four *amos* without tzitzis and tefillin, and I produced eighty students. And now my actions and Torah are the same as those of the butcher?!"

Rabbi Yehoshua was very upset about it. He told his students, "I must see who this person is and what he did to become my neighbor in Gan Eden." So Rabbi Yehoshua and his students went straight to that city and started looking for the butcher. When they found him, Rabbi Yehoshua asked him, "What do you do for a living and what do you do in life?" He said to him, "Your honor, I'm a butcher. My mother and father are very old and can't move around. So every day I dress them, feed them, and wash them with my own hands."

Rabbi Yehoshua immediately stood up, kissed him on his head, and said, "I am so honored to be your neighbor in Gan Eden."

This shows the incredible reward that a person gets for honoring his parents.

CHALLENGE FOR THE WEEK

When parents walk into the house or room, let's remember to stand up for them.

PARASHAS VAYAKHEL-PEKUDEI

Losing Out Because of Laziness

They were in the middle of an exciting game of cards. Reuven picked up a card and immediately put it on the pile. His sister picked up a card and put two down. Then it was Reuven's turn. He picked up a bad card and had to miss a turn. His sister was winning. In fact, she'd almost finished all of her cards!

At last, it was his turn again. Reuven picked up a card and was so excited. What a great card! Now he could get rid of three cards!

Their little brother was pushing around his tractor on the floor next to them. "Beep-beep-beep," he shouted and almost ran over Reuven's foot.

"Move away from here!" shouted Reuven. He looked back at his cards and tried to see if he could win this time.

All of a sudden, he heard his mother's voice: "Kids, who can come and help me please?"

Reuven picked up his card and was about to put it down on the

top of the pile. But then he noticed that his sister had stopped playing.

"Who's coming to help?" their mother called again.

Reuven wanted to keep on playing. His sister, though, had already put down her cards and got up to go to their mother.

"I'll carry on your turn," Reuven offered. She nodded and ran off.

Reuven continued the game but it was boring to play by himself. His little brother was also obviously fed up with playing with his tractor because he came over to Reuven and knocked over the whole pile of cards.

"Hey! Why did you do that?" Reuven grumbled and got up from his seat. Truthfully speaking, it didn't bother him that the cards were mixed up. He didn't want to keep on playing, anyway. He decided that he would go see what his mother needed.

"Imma, how can I help?" he asked.

His mother looked at him and smiled. "Thank you for asking. It's a little late, though," she said. "Maybe next time you'll get the mitzvah."

QUESTIONS FOR THE FAMILY

- What things stop a person from running to do a mitzvah?
- What things help a person to run to do a mitzvah?

It says in the *parashah*: "And the leaders brought the *shoham* stones" (*Shemos* 35:27).

Rashi asks, "Why did the leaders decide to be the first to contribute to the *Chanukas HaMizbei'ach*?" He explains that they missed out on helping with the construction of the *Mishkan*. In the end, they only gave *after* the Jewish People had already given almost everything; now they wanted to make up for their mistake and do it quickly this time.

This is what Rabbi Yehudah ben Teima meant when he said, "Be brave as a leopard, swift as an eagle, fast like a deer, and strong like a lion to do the will of your Father in heaven" (*Avos* 5:20).

But how can we be brave as a leopard, swift as an eagle, etc.? After all, each animal is unique. How can we ever copy every single animal?

The Malbim (*Bereishis* 2:19) writes that when Hashem created man, he took the unique quality of each animal and put it in man. A person therefore contains all the different qualities of all the animals. If he didn't have them inside him already, he wouldn't be expected to copy them. But now that he does, he must use all of them to serve Hashem.

For example, we got the quality of speed from the deer. Therefore, if we *want* to, we can do things very quickly. The *Baal HaTurim* writes that Naftali was known for being fast, like it says: "Naftali is like a wild deer that runs" (*Bereishis* 49:21). When Yaakov's sons were about to bury their father, Eisav tried to stop them and forced them to go get the contract from Egypt. Naftali, who was very quick, was chosen for the job because it needed to be done quickly.

The following story is from the book *Zerizim Memaharim L'Mitzvos* by Ariella Savir.

> Avraham's mother bought a pair of pants for Avraham but they needed to be shortened so that he could wear them for Shabbos. Avraham's mother was sick, though, and didn't have the strength to fix them.
>
> What would Avraham wear on Shabbos? He decided to ask his sister Miriam for help. "Would you be able to shorten them for me?" he asked. "Sure," replied Miriam. But then the yetzer hara came and whispered a terrible secret to Miriam. He said to her, "Tell him that you are very tired. That you are very sorry. Another time, though." Miriam listened to the yetzer hara and told him that she would shorten them, but at a different time.
>
> Avraham decided to ask his sister Rachel. "Of course," Rachel replied. But then the yetzer hara came and whispered a terrible

secret to Rachel. He said to her: "Tell him that you're very tired. That you're very sorry. Another time, though." Rachel listened to the yetzer hara and told him that she couldn't shorten them right then, but maybe she could do it later.

That night, Miriam suddenly remembered that her brother had asked her to sew his pants. She quickly grabbed a pair of scissors and shortened the pants. An hour later, Rachel also remembered that she had promised to fix the pants. She took them, made them shorter and put them back in their place.

On Shabbos morning, Avraham put on the pants and screamed, "What happened to my pants? Why do they only reach my knees? What am I going to do now?"

His sisters felt very bad for Avraham. They said to him, "We're very sorry. Next time, we'll try not to listen to the yetzer hara. If somebody asks us to do something, we'll go and do it right away because capable people run to do mitzvos."

CHALLENGE FOR THE WEEK

This week, let's try to do a mitzvah right away.
Try to remember how many you did.

PARASHAS VAYIKRA

What's Wrong with a Mess?

Yossi was about to leave for school when, all of a sudden, he remembered the teacher's warning. It was a good thing too that he remembered, because the teacher had warned Yossi that he would be sent home if he didn't bring his pencil case to school today.

Yossi went back to his room to look for his pencil case but he had no clue where it was. There were piles of stuff on the desk, the floor was a complete disaster, and his bed was a mess.

He went to his desk and started looking through the pile. As he searched, books fell on the floor, scribbled-on papers floated all over, and markers landed on the fresh pile next to his feet. Wait! Hey, look, the alarm clock! He'd been looking for it for three days—ever since his mother had done the weekly straightening up. The alarm clock also somehow fell on the ground and smashed into pieces. But Yossi didn't have time to pick up the pieces and try to put them back together again. He had to find the pencil case urgently!

At last, Yossi managed to track it down. He grabbed it excitedly—only to discover that the case was empty. All of the pencils and pens that used to be inside had disappeared and were nowhere to be found. Where could they be?

On the floor, there was a pile of all sorts of clothes, games, Shabbos shoes, his one lost slipper, and lots of other items that he had completely forgotten about. All of a sudden, a pen fell out of the pocket of one of the shirts. Yossi picked it up and checked to see if it worked.

As expected, it didn't work. And even though the alarm clock had broken when it fell, the clock on the wall kept ticking away. Yossi got a shock when he noticed how late it was.

He was so upset that he kicked the messy pile with his foot. Not only had all his pens and pencils disappeared in all the mess. In a second, he was about to lose his mind too!

QUESTIONS FOR THE FAMILY

- Does this ever happen to you?
- Can you give an example of something that you needed but couldn't find?

It says in the *parashah*: "If a soul sins…" (*Vayikra* 4:2).

The *Midrash* (*Vayikra Rabbah* 4:5) on this *pasuk* uses the following *mashal* to describe the battle between the *yetzer hatov* and the *yetzer hara*.

Rabbi Yishmael explained: This can be compared to a king who had an orchard that was full of beautiful fruit. To protect it,

the king hired two guards: one who was crippled and one who was blind. He told them, "You must guard all this beautiful fruit." After a few days, the cripple said to the blind man, "I see such beautiful fruit in the orchard." The blind person said to him, "Go get some and we'll eat." The cripple said to him, "But I can't walk!" The blind person said, "And I can't see!" The cripple climbed onto the blind man's shoulders and they went and ate the fruit. Then they went back to their places and sat down.

Later on, the king came to visit the orchard and said to them, "Where's all the beautiful fruit?" The blind person said: "Your Royal Highness, can I see?" The cripple said: "Your Royal Highness, can I walk?" The king was very smart. He knew exactly what to do. He lifted the cripple onto the blind person's shoulders and told them to "walk around." Then he said to them, "You see. This is what you did and this is how you managed to get the fruit."

This is what Hashem will say to the soul in the future: "Why did you sin against Me?" The soul will say to Him, "Master of the World, I didn't sin. The body is the one that sinned. Ever since I left him, I'm like an innocent bird flying in the sky. What did I do wrong?" Then Hashem will say to the body, "Why did you sin against Me?" The body will say to Him, "Master of the World, I didn't sin. The soul is the one that sinned. Ever since it left me, I've been lying like a stone that fell on the ground. What did I do wrong?" So what will Hashem do to them? He will take the soul and throw it into the body and judge them together—like one being."

Every now and again, every person feels that there is a fight going on inside him. First the *yetzer hara* whispers something to him. Then the *yetzer hatov* whispers the opposite. A person is like a horse with a rider. But he has to decide if he wants to let the horse lead him or if he wants to lead the horse.

It's the same idea when it comes to living in a mess. A child is like the rider. He has to make sure that his room is neat. Sometimes, though, the "horse" pulls him away to go play or read, instead of tidying up. Then the child has to try to fight back against this feeling and control it.

The *Saba* of Kelm once went to visit his son who was learning in the Volozhener Yeshiva. The first thing that he did was to go into the dormitory where his son was staying. When he walked out of the building, he went straight back to Kelm, without even going into the yeshiva and asking about how his son was doing. When asked why he didn't, the *Saba* explained, "When I saw how neat and tidy my son's room was, I knew that my son was also organized in the way that he served Hashem and learned Torah."

CHALLENGE FOR THE WEEK
This week, let's make a special effort to keep our rooms neat.

PARASHAS TZAV

Eating Respectably

During recess, all of the students got into groups on the floor to play marbles as usual. Yossi rolled the marbles and won one round after the other. But then he was out. One marble had unexpectedly spun away under a desk and he went to pick it up. In the meantime, it was Yehudah's turn.

Yossi sat on the floor and watched his friends play. Then he remembered that he had an apple in his bag. He got up and went to get the apple. Instead of coming back to sit on the floor, he preferred to watch the game from where he could see better, so he sat down on the desk nearby.

He sat there happily and munched on his apple. But his friend Reuven didn't look so happy with him. "You're not allowed to sit on a desk," criticized Reuven loudly. "You should know that a desk is like a mizbei'ach." Yossi didn't appreciate the rebuke, especially because Reuven told him this while he himself was eating a piece of cake in a very unappealing way. In fact, it was so disgusting to watch him eat that Yossi looked away and said, "There are also other halachos about

eating, such as how to put food in one's mouth and not make a mess!"

"There are halachos like those?" asked Reuven in a very mocking tone as he wiped his crumb-filled hands on his shirt. "Really?"

Just then, the rebbi walked into the classroom. "Of course there are halachos about eating," he told them. "Let's sit down and learn what's written about this subject in the Kitzur Shulchan Aruch."

QUESTION FOR THE FAMILY

Can you give examples of how to eat respectably?

The *mizbei'ach* was where the *korbanos* were burned by a holy fire and offered up to Hashem. Unfortunately, we don't have the Beis Hamikdash or the *mizbei'ach* now. We do have something instead, though.

The *Shelah HaKadosh* writes that a person's table is like a *mizbei'ach*, and the food that we eat on it is instead of a *korban*. And what's instead of the fire? The *divrei Torah* that we say at the table. When we eat correctly, our eating is like the service in the Beis Hamikdash.

How does one eat correctly? A person should sit respectably at the table because he is eating at the King's table. One should not stuff himself with food, nor speak with food in his mouth. A person should also make sure to say the *berachos* properly. He should also say *divrei Torah* at the table, as that makes the food holy, like the fire that came down from heaven and burned the offerings.

A person should imagine that all the heavenly angels are watching how he "brings his offering." If he crams all the food into his mouth in a disgusting way, wouldn't all the heavenly angels be shocked to see him behaving like an animal?! We need to remember that each of us is a prince or princess, a child of the King of all kings, and a truly important person always eats respectably.

The great sage Rabbi Isser Zalman Meltzer, zt"l, Rosh Yeshiva of Yeshivas Eitz Chaim in Yerushalayim, would often go to Chevron to *daven* at the *kevarim* of the *Avos*. A few of the top students at his yeshiva would go with him on these trips. On these occasions, he would take them along to visit the *Saba* of Slabodka, who lived in Chevron. When he arrived on one of his visits to the *Saba*, Rabbi Isser Zalman announced: "I have brought the greatest of all of my students with me today! This is the *ilui* over whom everyone will eventually make a huge fuss!" The *Saba* greeted them warmly and invited them to join him at the table. He asked the Rebbetzin to bring cups of tea as well as sugar for the guests. The three sat and discussed different Torah subjects. All of a sudden, the *Saba* noticed that the young *ilui* was picking up sugar granules with his fingertips and licking them. The *Saba* was very unimpressed because he saw this as a lack of *derech eretz*. He felt that this was not the way to behave among *talmidei chachamim*. In order not to make him feel bad, though, the *Saba* just kept quiet.

At the end of the visit, the *Saba* turned toward the young man and said to him, "I would like to ask you a few questions. Please tell me who is more important—a living person or a dead person?" The young man was surprised by the question and answered, "The living person, of course." Then the *Saba* asked, "Which is more important—a living lion or a dead lion?" The *ilui* answered right away, "It's obvious that the living lion is more important." The *Saba* wasn't done asking. His next question was, "Which is more important—a living dog or a dead dog?" The *ilui* said, "The living dog." The *Saba* asked another question, "Which of the two is more important—a living dog or a dead lion?" The young man answered, "There is a *pasuk* that clearly says: 'The living dog is better than the dead lion.'" The *Saba* said, "I'd like to end off by giving you a riddle. Can you think of when a dead carcass is better than a living person?" The *ilui* answered right away, "No. It can't be."

"Even though it's only a riddle, you're wrong. Chazal (*Vayikra Rabba* 1) say that any *talmid chacham* who lacks *da'as* is worse than a dead carcass." Rabbi Isser Zalman understood immediately what this comment was referring to. *Da'as* refers to *derech eretz*, and the *Saba* was hinting that the young man had behaved without *derech eretz*. When the *ilui* left the room for a few minutes, Rabbi Isser Zalman said to the *Saba*: "With all due respect, I think that the *Saba* exaggerated. I already mentioned that this young man is a first-rate *ilui* and will go very far in life!" But the *Saba* wasn't convinced and said, "The fact that he licked the sugar shows that he has to work on himself. If he doesn't improve, he won't be anyone at all. In fact, he won't even be connected to those who dedicate their lives to the Torah!" Rabbi Isser Zalman disagreed and said, "I still think that the *Saba* is making a mistake."

When Rabbi Meir Chodosh, *zt"l*, used to tell this story to his students, he would finish with the following words, "I knew this *ilui* when he was young. And I also knew him when he was much older. And I can testify that this person grew up and unfortunately the *Saba* was right."

This idea is clearly written in the Mishnah (*Avos* 3:21): "If there is no *derech eretz*, there is no Torah." *Rabbeinu Yonah* explains this as follows: "This means that a person has to first improve himself, and then the Torah will dwell in him. The Torah will never come to a person who doesn't have good *middos*."

CHALLENGE FOR THE WEEK
This week, let's make sure that we eat respectably.

PARASHAS SHEMINI

Dealing with Jealousy

Yossi came home from school feeling down. His mother noticed right away that he was sad. But Yossi didn't say a word about it. In fact, when she asked him how his day was at school, Yossi answered, "All right."

Yossi's mother knew, though, that everything was not right, and definitely not all right. Yossi sat down on the sofa, doing nothing at all. He didn't read, draw, or play. He didn't even speak. This behavior seemed very strange.

"Are you feeling okay, Yossi?" she asked.

"Yes," he said.

"I mean, in your heart," she said with a smile.

Yossi gave her a half-hearted smile in return. "Not really," he admitted.

"What happened?" his mother inquired.

Yossi hesitated for a moment and said, "He's better than me in everything—in everything! He knows everything better than everyone else. He understands everything that the rebbi says and always asks the best questions. All the teachers are so impressed with him and give him compliments all the time. Also, he gets top grades on all the tests, even the hardest ones."

Then Yossi stopped talking. His mother asked him gently, "Did you get back any tests today?"

"Yes," said Yossi and he took out a piece of paper that had been folded quite a few times. "We had a test in Mishnah. And I didn't get such a good grade...but Gadi got a hundred!" said Yossi, very upset. "A hundred percent! He showed his test to quite a few kids and announced his grade to everybody. This really made me mad because I didn't get a good grade."

Yossi didn't say exactly what grade he got and Imma didn't pressure him to tell her.

"He's got everything," continued Yossi, "Treats, new games, and also these designer clothes. Even...he even has good mid-dos. Yeah, he's like the perfect kid. Why does one boy have all the right things and the other kid has nothing?"

Yossi became quiet again. His mother also didn't say anything. After a while, Yossi looked up and then said shyly, "I think that I'm really jealous of him."

"It's good that you really understand what you are feeling," his mother said. "And it's very good that you know how to express them in such a grown-up way. This also helps you to work on this middah. You've got a lot going for you! Many adults still get jealous and it makes them feel pretty bad. But you're young and already know that, so you're doing great."

QUESTIONS FOR THE FAMILY

- Do you also get jealous sometimes? About what?
- How can a person stop being jealous?

In this week's *parashah*, it says: "And a fire came from Hashem and burned them, and they died before Hashem" (*Vayikra* 10:2).

This is quite surprising. What sin did Nadav and Avihu do that they deserved to die?

The Gemara (*Sanhedrin* 52b) says that when Nadav and Avihu walked behind Moshe and Aharon, they said to each other: "When are these two elderly leaders going to die and then you and I will be in charge of the people?" The *Maharsha* explains that they were jealous.

Chazal describe how bad it is to be jealous. It is such a terrible *middah* that it says: "Envy is the [cause of] rotting of bones" (*Mishlei* 14:30). It also says: "Jealousy, lust, and [the desire for] honor remove a person from the world" (*Avos* 4:28). Also, jealousy doesn't help at all because Hashem gives a person whatever he needs. And if he doesn't have something that somebody else has, then this means that he doesn't need it.

Rabbi Aharon Kotler, *zt"l*, once had a student whose wife passed away. Her funeral was scheduled to be abroad, but it was delayed because it was both Shabbos and *yom tov*. In the meantime, her family tried to look for a way to keep her body cold so that it wouldn't decompose. Her husband, however, said, "There's no need for refrigeration because I can testify that she was never jealous of anyone else. She was always generous, without even a trace of envy; her body won't rot at all. And the *pasuk* tells us that a person's bones only rot if he was jealous." They didn't refrigerate her body and nothing happened to her. What an incredible miracle!

The Gemara (*Shabbos* 152b) tells a story about a group of people who dug in Rav Nachman's field and discovered a grave. Rav Achai, the person who was buried there, shouted at them. They came to Rav Nachman and told him that a dead person had shouted at them. Rav Nachman went and asked him, "Who are you, sir?" The dead person said, "I am Achai, the son of Yoshiya." Rav Nachman then asked, "How could it be that your body is intact? Rav Achai answered, "It says: 'Envy is the [cause of] rotting of bones,' which means that if someone is jealous while he is alive, then his bones will rot afterward. I wasn't jealous, though, so my bones are still intact."

CHALLENGE FOR THE WEEK

Let's try not to be jealous of other people's talents, accomplishments, or possessions.

PARASHAS TAZRIA-METZORA

Having a Generous Nature

"Hey, tomorrow is Imma's birthday!"

Yossi dropped the fork all of a sudden. Pieces of cucumber and tomato juice flew across the table. But he didn't even notice that the table was a mess. All he cared was that, fortunately, he had remembered the birthday.

Every year, the older children would buy a small present for their mother. The girls would wrap the gift beautifully and add notes containing warm wishes. This project was always done secretly so that Imma wouldn't notice the surprise. The preparations would carry on for several days and all the children would help out. Only the youngest children wouldn't be included. It was too difficult to rely on them to keep it secret.

This year, though, they hadn't done anything.

Yossi immediately realized why. Their oldest brother was currently in yeshiva. He only came home once a month. And nobody besides him would remember the date and get everybody involved.

This was his chance to really make himself look good. Yossi was so excited that he kept on eating without even looking at what

he was eating. He had never ever dared to taste peanut butter. And now he'd already eaten a whole slice of bread smeared with peanut butter without even noticing that he was eating it.

He was so busy thinking about this project, which he wanted to do all by himself. This time, he would get the present ready from beginning to end. He would use his own money to buy a nice, practical gift. He would ask the person at the store to wrap it beautifully. He would write a birthday wish on fancy paper. He would do everything by himself.

He would be the only one who remembered their mother's birthday. He would also be the only one who would get the compliments when she got the present.

*The plan seemed perfect. Yossi was about to bentch and go to the store. But then a thought popped into his head: Wait! Why **shouldn't** everybody be included?*

It was true that the other children had forgotten this important date. But why not let them know about it? This way, they could all arrange the present together. Like they always did. He realized that then he wouldn't get all the credit. But he knew that it was much better to have everybody involved. This would also save his brothers and sisters from being embarrassed because they forgot.

He started bentching and then went to call everybody to a secret meeting in the children's room...

QUESTIONS FOR THE FAMILY

- Which good *middah* does Yossi have?
- Can you give an example of using an *ayin tovah* (generous nature) and not being stingy?

Chazal (*Arachin* 16a) say that there are seven things that can cause a person to be punished with *tzara'as*.

> Rav Shmuel bar Nachmani says that Rabbi Yochanan said: "People get skin diseases because of harmful words, murder, taking an oath for no reason, immorality, haughtiness, theft, and stinginess."

From the entire list mentioned above, stinginess seems to be the exception. This is because being stingy doesn't seem as bad as the other sins that are on the list.

Let's try to understand why the Torah thinks that this character flaw is so terrible and why it causes diseases to come to the world.

When the Torah talks about a house that gets a plague, the *pasuk* says, "And the one to whom the house *belongs*" (*Vayikra* 14:35). *Tana D'Bei Rabbi Yishmael* explains: "The one whose house is only *his*." The Gemara (*Yoma* 11b) explains that this refers to somebody who keeps his home only for himself.

A stingy person refuses to lend his items to his neighbors by pretending that he doesn't have things they ask for. As a result, Hashem will make his house get *tzara'as*. The person will then be forced to take everything out of his house, and all the things that he refused to lend out will be available for everyone to see.

We must try to stay away from stinginess and try to always give and share.

Rabbi Yehonasan Eibeshitz, *zt"l*, married the daughter of a wealthy man. When they got married, her father gave them three thousand gold coins as a gift. After the wedding, he devoted himself to learning Torah day and night. He and his *chavrusa* would sit and learn together in the *beis midrash* for hours and hours.

At that time, the local Christians decided to build a church directly facing the *beis midrash*. They even put a large and very noticeable cross on top. This really bothered everyone in the *beis midrash*, especially Rabbi

Yehonasan's *chavrusa*, who had a very bad temper. He got so angry about it that one night he climbed onto the roof of the church and broke the cross.

People found out about it and caught him. A short time later, the non-Jewish caretaker of the church made a secret offer to one of the leaders of the Jewish community. He said that he was prepared to help the Jew escape, but because it was extremely dangerous, he demanded three thousand gold coins as payment. The Jewish community heard about the huge sum that was required and offered to collect the money to redeem their fellow Jew from jail.

When the news reached Rabbi Yehonasan, he went home and brought the exact amount of money to the church caretaker. No one else knew that he did this. The caretaker kept his promise and helped the Jew to escape. The Jew ran away and went to live in a different city.

In the meantime, the *gabba'ei tzedakah* continued to try to raise the entire sum of money. When they came to Rabbi Yehonasan, they told him that they had only managed to collect part of the amount. He told them that the money was no longer necessary. That's when an argument broke out between the *gabba'ei tzedakah* and Rabbi Yehonasan. They said, "Even though you already gave the whole amount, we still collected whatever we could in the meantime. We didn't get the entire three thousand gold coins, but we still deserve to share in the mitzvah." But Rabbi Yehonasan refused to include them in this mitzvah.

At the same time, Rabbi Yehonasan began to think about what would happen when his wife found out that he gave away their entire fortune. She would be furious!

He decided that he would leave the city for a few days. Hopefully, she would discover that the money was missing while he was away. She would then probably think that somebody had broken into their home and stolen the money. And by the time Rabbi Yehonasan would come back home, she would have calmed down and accepted the loss.

He went and told his wife that he wanted to go away for a few days to take care of an important issue in a faraway city. Meanwhile, the priests discovered that the Jew, who had been sentenced to death, had escaped. It didn't take long for them to realize that it was the church caretaker who had betrayed them and helped the Jew to escape. They got together and decided that the caretaker should get the punishment they'd intended to give to the Jew. The caretaker realized what was about to happen and decided to run away.

Besides being greedy, the caretaker was also a very experienced thief. In the past, he had managed to steal a lot of gold and silver from the church. He took all his riches and ran to the home of Rabbi Yehonasan. He told the Rebbetzin everything that had happened and said to her, "Your husband is a brave Jew. He gave three thousand gold coins from his own money in order to save his friend. That's why I'm sure that he's an honest and trustworthy person. Here are the three thousand gold coins as a present. I'm also leaving this chest, which is full of gold, with you."

Now Rabbi Yehonasan's wife knew about the entire incident. She recognized that Hashem had paid them back for the kind, charitable act that her husband had done, and she waited anxiously for her husband to return so that she could tell him the incredible news.

When Rabbi Yehonasan arrived home, his wife was so excited. She said, "Hashem paid us back many times over," and told him the whole story.

The Rabbi listened, but instead of dancing with joy, he burst out crying. His wife stood there in shock and couldn't understand what happened. When Rabbi Yehonasan calmed down, he explained, "I'm crying because I realized that Heaven is not happy with the mitzvah that I did. If they were happy with it, then they would have paid me back in the World to Come. That's because it's well-known that the reward for a mitzvah is only given in the World to Come. Reward is only given in this world if the mitzvah is *not* wanted."

Rabbi Yehonasan cried and cried. Eventually, he decided to do a three-day fast to find out why Heaven wasn't pleased with the mitzvah that he did. This is the answer that he got: "It's all because you were stingy with the mitzvah of redeeming your friend and didn't let the rest of the community also share in the mitzvah."

CHALLENGE FOR THE WEEK
This week, let's try to include others in a mitzvah that we're doing.

Loving One's Fellow Jew

Yossi walked into his house. It was very loud and busy. His brother had brought a few friends home and they were building a huge city from pieces of different games. There were houses made of Clics, roads made from Kapla blocks, all sorts of buildings made from Lego pieces, as well as cars, miniature people, and more.

As his brother ran back and forth, Yossi watched him from the side. He sure was full of life—energetic, happy, and very active.

The friends chatted excitedly among themselves and Imma offered them cookies and juice.

Yossi took one more look at them and then went to his room and lay on the bed with a book. After reading for a minute, he closed it and said, "Ach, what a boring book! What can I do now?"

He thought about going downstairs and riding on his bike for a while.

He looked out the window. Some of his classmates were right outside but he wasn't in the mood to play with them. Shimon was an annoying type of kid. As for Reuven, Yossi couldn't stand

him at all. In fact, he hated him. And Gadi, too, was a goody-goody, always smiling at everyone and trying to please them.

No, he really didn't feel like going to play with them.

Then he spotted Yehudah. What? Yehudah was also there? Then he definitely wasn't going to go down. Yehudah was the one he liked the least in the class. He was one of those kids who considered himself to be a know-it-all. He was always finding something to rebuke other people about and give them plenty of criticism.

With "friends" like these, it was better to stay home and be bored.

QUESTIONS FOR THE FAMILY

- Do you have to be friends with everyone in your class?
- How can we love other Jews more?

In the *parashah*, it says: "And you must love your fellow Jew." Rashi comments: "Rabbi Akiva says: 'This is a key principle in the Torah'" (*Vayikra* 19:18).

The Gemara in *Maseches Shabbos* (31a) tells us that there once was a non-Jew who came to Hillel the Elder and said, "I want to convert and become a Jew but only on one condition—that you teach me the entire Torah while I stand on one foot." Hillel looked at him fondly and told him, "Whatever you don't like, don't do to your friend."

The author of the *Chiddushei HaRim* asked: Why didn't Hillel teach him the principle "You must love your fellow man"? Why did he tell him what he *shouldn't* do?

He answered that the non-Jew wouldn't be able to fully absorb the idea of loving one's fellow man. He wouldn't understand how it's possible to love someone else as much as himself, but he could relate to the idea of not harming another person. This is like the saying: "Live and let live." Don't bother your friend, just as you don't want him to bother you. That is why, when Hillel wanted to teach that non-Jew, he had to speak to him in his own language.

One evening, the community leaders came to meet with the great Brisker Rav. It was very cold in his home. They went to the Rebbetzin and asked her, "Didn't we fill up your shed with wood yesterday?" The Rebbetzin replied, "Yes, but yesterday a lot of poor people came to us and complained that they didn't have wood. The Rav felt that he simply had to help them, so he gave all the wood to them and there was none left for us."

The community leaders went and restocked the shed with wood. But this time, they gave the key to the Rebbetzin so that she would lock it up and not give it to the Rav. They even warned her, "If the Rav gives the wood to poor people, it's as if he's stealing."

The community leaders came the next day and discovered that the house was cold—again. "Did you give the key to the Rav?" they asked the Rebbetzin. "No," she told them. "Then why is it cold here?" the leaders asked. The Rebbetzin answered, "The Rav said that if the poor people would have to suffer from the cold, then so would we!"

That's what it means to really care about other people. By the way, the community got the message and made sure that the poor people also got wood.

How does a person work on loving his fellow Jew?

Rabbi Eliyahu Eliezer Dessler writes that giving to someone helps you to love him. As Chazal said, "If you want to connect to [the concept of] loving your fellow man, get busy helping him."

Rabbi Dessler writes that he saw this idea with his own eyes. There was a young couple who had an only son and he was the light of their lives. But then a war broke out in that area and everybody had to escape from the fighting. It so happened that the couple went different ways—the father and his son to one location and the mother to a different location. They didn't meet for several years, but throughout those years the mother never stopped yearning for her little boy. When the war ended and the family was reunited, the joy was beyond belief. The mother was finally back together again with her beloved son, the darling of her life.

We would expect to see from that point onward that the loving relationship between the mother and her child would be greater and more intense than that of the father. This is because there was no change for the father with regard to his child, whereas the mother had to make up for all those years of longing for her son. Surprisingly though, the father's love for the boy was much **more** intense and passionate than the mother's. She had left him when he was a little boy and reunited with him as an adult. From her perspective, this was a different child. She still wanted to be with the little boy from whom she had been separated a long time ago.

What happened? Rabbi Dessler explains that throughout the war years, the father was busy day and night with how to protect his child. He helped his child to survive in the most difficult situations and gave him so much. As a result, the bond and the love grew tremendously and became ingrained in him. On the other hand, the mother missed out on those years of giving, and this created a gap between them. We see that the more we give to someone, the more we will learn to care about them.

There is a story about two close friends who loved each other very much. One day, they were falsely accused and sentenced to be hanged to death. On the day on which the sentence was scheduled to be carried out, the entire city gathered in the city center. The king and some of the important members of the city also came to the event. As the sentence was about to be carried out, one friend shouted, "Stop! Stop! He's innocent. I'm the one who's guilty, not him." When the other friend heard this, he also started shouting, "No, I'm guilty!" until a huge tumult arose.

The king called for the two of them and asked them to explain what happened. They said to him, "Your Majesty the King, the truth is that both of us are innocent and all of this is a conspiracy. Since we love each other so much, though, each of us was prepared to give up our lives for the other one." The king listened and said to them, "If so, I also want to be a part of this incredible friendship that you have."

This is what it means when it says: "And you shall love your friend like yourself—I am Hashem."

CHALLENGE FOR THE WEEK

This week, let's try to do something good for a person whom we don't like so much.

Let's try to help him, ask him how he's doing, or daven for him to be successful.

PARASHAS EMOR

Not Making Other People Feel Bad

At the Shabbos table, Yossi just wasn't in the mood. He didn't know why. There wasn't any specific reason, that's just how it was.

It wasn't like anything was missing that Shabbos. Yossi wore his favorite white shirt, the one with the square buttons. His mother served his favorite salads at the table. The challah was fresh and yummy, and the fish was also delicious. There was lots of soda on the table, and the candies, which he got from the gabbai after davening, were waiting for him in his pocket.

But for some reason, he just didn't want to sing at the table.

Yossi looked at the words of the Shabbos zemiros. He listened as his father sang while his younger brother tried to sing along in his squeaky voice. His brother didn't know how to pronounce the Aramaic words properly and after a few lines, he gave up and stopped singing.

Their father continued singing by himself.

"Nu," he winked at Yossi, but Yossi pretended as if he didn't get the hint. He kept staring down at the white tablecloth and didn't say a word.

The song ended. Yossi breathed a sigh of relief and lifted up his head. That's when he looked at his father.

Yossi's father didn't seem angry, nor did he blame Yossi. He had a different look in his eyes—sort of disappointed and sad.

Yossi felt so bad. He didn't know what was going on with himself. What had happened to him? Why didn't he join in the singing? He had made his father sad for no reason. What a pity.

Yossi decided that he would try to change his mood. Fortunately, there were still more zemiros to be sung at the Shabbos table. When his father would start singing again in a little while, he would join him. Then the two of them could sing and harmonize together—just as they did every Shabbos.

QUESTIONS FOR THE FAMILY

- Do you try to make other people happy?
- Do you like to sing with other people?

It says in the *parashah*: "And they put him [the blasphemer] in jail so that they could find out [how to punish him]" (*Vayikra* 24:12). Rashi explains: "They locked him up by himself and did not put the person who collected the wood in the same jail as him. They did this because both of these incidents occurred at the same period of time and they knew that the person who collected the wood would be put to death." The *Sifsei Chachamim* explains that if they would have put them together, the blasphemer would think that he was going to be put to death just like the person who collected the wood. Since it was possible that the blasphemer wouldn't actually be killed, he would have worried for no reason.

We learn an important lesson from this incident. The Torah was so careful to make sure that the wicked blasphemer would not suffer, even though it wasn't even clear that he would be upset. How much more so should we be extra careful not to make anyone else feel upset or sad in any way.

The *Chiddushei HaLev* asks the following question: It's still difficult to understand! Why didn't they put the blasphemer and wood collector together and just tell the blasphemer that they didn't know yet whether he would get the death penalty? The answer may be that they were worried that the blasphemer wouldn't believe them. He might have thought that they'd put him together with the wood collector because he *would* get the death penalty like him.

We see from this how careful we have to be not to make other people feel sad or suffer.

We also find this type of conduct with respect to Hashem. When Yosef was sold to the Yishmaelim, it says: "And their camels were carrying various spices and balsam" (*Bereishis* 37:25). Why? Rashi explains: "To show the reward that is given to *tzaddikim*. It's true that Arabs usually carry oil and tar, which smell really bad. But Hashem made sure that there would be pleasant spices so that Yosef wouldn't be harmed by the terrible odor."

This teaches us about Hashem's ways. Even though it was decided in Heaven that Yosef had to suffer, it was carefully measured out so that he shouldn't suffer more than he had to.

One day, a *talmid chacham* came to the home of Rav Shlomo Zalman Auerbach to invite him to his son's bar mitzvah. Rav Auerbach gave him a *berachah* but apologized that he would not be able to come because he already had two *simchahs* that he had to go to on the same day.

On the day of the bar mitzvah, the father was surprised to see that Rav Auerbach had come. Rav Auerbach explained to him as follows: "I remembered that I had come to the bar mitzvahs of all your other sons, and I was worried that this son would be upset if I didn't come to his bar mitzvah. That's why I made a special effort to be here. I wanted to make sure that he would be happy."

There is a story about Rabbi Yisrael Salanter who noticed a broken shutter on one of the houses when he lived in the city of Salant. He was worried that the broken shutter would disturb or upset the neighbors, or wake them up at night, so he quickly went and made sure that it was fixed immediately.

CHALLENGE FOR THE WEEK

Let's try to make other people happy. How do you think we can do that?

Next week, let's discuss how we did!

PARASHAS BEHAR-BECHUKOSAI

Caring for Others
Who Have Less

Yossi had done really well today. He won all the games that he played during recess. Now his box was so full of marbles that there was hardly any more space inside. He couldn't wait to go home and count them all; he felt like a king!

He closed the box tightly and put it in a packet so that nothing would fall out. That's when he noticed Reuven.

Reuven sat quietly in his place and watched the boys playing. Marbles flew in all directions. Shouting and excitement were heard from every corner. But Reuven just sat there all alone, as if all the noise didn't affect him at all.

"Where are your marbles?" asked Yossi. He had seen Reuven that morning with a box that was quite full.

Reuven pointed sadly to an empty box that sat on the chair next to him. "They're finished," he said quietly.

"You lost everything?" said Yossi, quite surprised.

Reuven nodded.

"Poor guy," thought Yossi. He felt so sad for him. That's when he stood up, walked into the middle of the crowd, and announced: "We're doing a collection! Who can donate marbles to a friend who doesn't have any?"

He didn't tell anybody which friend it was. Even when some of the boys begged him to tell them, he refused. He just kept on yelling, "Who's donating marbles to the collection?"

Yossi took the empty box and walked around all the kids. He tried to get everybody to share in this special opportunity to do tzedakah. "The poor people of your city come first," he shouted, "and for sure, the poor people of your class!"

And the marbles started pouring into the box.

At the end of recess, he gave the jam-packed box to Reuven. He felt so good when he saw the sparkle in Reuven's eyes as he took all those marbles.

QUESTIONS FOR THE FAMILY

- Do you help out other people?
- How?

It says in the *parashah*: "If your fellow Jew becomes poor and loses his possessions…you must give him support…so that he can live with you" (*Vayikra* 25:35).

It also says in *Midrash Rabbah* 35: Rabbi Abbin says, "The beggar stands at your door and Hashem stands to his right, as it says, 'Because He will stand to the right of the poor person.' If you give him, then remember that Hashem is standing on his right-hand side and will pay you back."

If a person helps a poor person, it's as if he's lending to Hashem

because Hashem looks after people. So if a person becomes poor and you come and do the mitzvah, then it is considered as if you're "helping" Hashem.

Imagine if a rich person would come and ask us to lend some money to a poor person for a few days. Wouldn't we give it to the poor person right away? Especially if we knew that the rich person would definitely pay us back and even consider us his partner.

Why shouldn't we think like that about Hashem? Hashem decides that some people should be poor so that we can support them. And when we do, then we get rewarded incredibly—and not from a human king, but rather from the King of all kings, Hashem Himself!

Which one of us wouldn't want an unbelievable gift like this?

Unfortunately, some people think that if they give away some of their money, they'll have less. They don't understand that this is like using one candle to light another candle. In the end, both candles stay lit. The same thing happens when we lend to a poor person. By helping the poor person, Hashem will certainly make sure that we don't lose out, even if we don't see it at that moment.

There was once a *talmid chacham* who spent a lot of time and effort doing *hachnasas orchim*. His friends asked him, "But isn't learning Torah equal to all the mitzvos?"

He answered them: "Let me tell you something and then you'll understand."

> *A while ago, I got very, very sick. All of a sudden, I felt my neshamah going up to the Heavenly court and they started judging me.*
>
> *But then I saw an old man come over and give a piece of paper to the judges. After they read the note, they decided that I could go back down to the world.*
>
> *I left the Heavenly court but didn't know where to go. Just then, that same old man appeared and said to me, "Come, I'll show you the way."*
>
> *I asked him, "Who are you?"*

He said to me, "I'll tell you. Sixty years ago, when you were a little boy, I happened to come to your city. The custom in your city was that every Jew would take a poor person home with him after davening on Friday night. My clothes smelled terrible, so nobody wanted to have me as a guest. I just stood there, all alone.

"You and your father were the last to leave shul. I saw that you asked your father to take me home with you. Your father told you that he wasn't prepared to, because I smelled so bad. You went home and I was left by myself at the shul.

"When you got home, you said to everyone, 'If you don't let the beggar come eat with us, then I won't eat either.' So they sent you to call me and I ate with your family. That meal saved my life because I hadn't eaten for a few days.

"Soon after that, I passed away. But I wanted to repay you for the kind deed that you did. When you came to beis din today, they sentenced you to death. That's why I came to you—to help defend you. I wrote a note and gave it to them, and this is what I wrote: Master of the World! You know that if someone keeps a Jew alive, it's as if he kept the entire world alive."

The *talmid chacham* ended his unbelievable story by saying, "And that's why they gave me more time in this world: just for being kind and helping a beggar. So how can I take a break from doing *chessed*?"

CHALLENGE FOR THE WEEK

This week, let's look for ways to help out somebody who really needs help.

Being Organized

"I'm so tired!" Dovid gave a big yawn. "I don't even have any energy to move."

"You really need to go to sleep," Dovid's mother said. "Why don't you go right now?"

Dovid dragged himself to his room, opened the door and did not like what he saw. The floor was covered with things, and so was his bed. How could he go to sleep like this?

He flopped down onto the bed and just lay there. Using his feet, he then pushed everything onto the floor. Clothes, books, and games landed with a thud. At least his bed was clear now.

Wait a minute! Where were his pajamas?

Dovid rummaged around by his pillow. No, there was nothing there. Well, his pajamas weren't there but there were some cards, pieces of crayon, and two batteries.

So where were his pajamas?

He knew that his mother wouldn't let him go to sleep with his

clothes on. So, even though he was exhausted, he sat up and went to look for his striped shirt and pants.

Dovid started searching through the mess on the floor. In the pile next to his bed, all that he managed to find was his sleeping kippah. Next to the desk, he found the clothes from yesterday and the test that he was supposed to get signed by his parents and then bring back to school today. He also looked through the clutter under the desk but didn't find the pajamas there either.

Gosh, where were his pajamas?

Maybe he could take a different set from the closet? He thought. He opened the cupboard but the shelf was empty. No pajamas at all. Where were the ones with the dots? And where was the black-and-white set? He probably forgot to put them in the laundry basket. And if the clothes weren't in the laundry, then they wouldn't get washed. That was the rule in their house.

So what happened to his pajamas? Maybe there was a mouse wandering around the room that liked to eat different colored pajamas? He didn't think so. He knew that he had taken off his pajamas that morning. He just couldn't remember where he'd put them...

QUESTIONS FOR THE FAMILY

- Is your room usually organized?
- Why do you think your room should be organized?
- Do you think that Hashem is happy when your room is organized or that He doesn't care?

It says in the *Midrash Rabbah* on this week's *parashah* that Hashem loved the Jewish People so much that he made flags for them. He gave each tribe its own flag in the color of the stone that was embedded in the *Choshen HaMishpat* that Aharon HaKohen wore. In this way, each tribe could be recognized from far away. Everyone knew that this was the tribe of Reuven, this was the tribe of Shimon, and so forth. All of this was out of Hashem's love for the Jews, as it says: "He brought me to the wine cellar and His flag over me is love"—the flags of the Jewish People were a sign of His love.

In addition to having their own flags, the Jews were also distinguished by the **order** in which they traveled and carried the *aron ha'bris*. Everything was done in an incredibly systematic and organized way. Each family, their animals, and their baggage—all of them—always traveled and camped in a neat and impressive formation, as it says: "Each person according to his flag with the insignias." The way in which they traveled was a sign and shining example to all the nations. It was so amazing that Chazal say that the nations of the world would stare at the Jewish People and wonder out loud, "Who is this that looks as beautiful as the dawn?" (*Shir HaShirim* 6:10). Even Bilaam, who wanted to curse the Jewish People, was impressed. When he saw how well they were arranged, he said, "Who can harm these people?"

Every aspect of the camping and carrying of the *Mishkan* and its utensils during the journeys in the desert was also according to a specific order. Every single Jew knew exactly what he had to do and how he should travel.

All this teaches us how a Jew should serve Hashem in everything that he does. A person's life has to be planned and organized. Then, when a person manages to achieve his goals, he'll know that he is serving Hashem correctly. But if he doesn't get organized, he won't be successful, *chas v'shalom*.

The *Saba* of Slabodka used to say that being organized is like the *knot in a string of pearls*. Even though it's true that the pearls are more precious than the knot, if the knot comes undone, then all the pearls will fall on the floor.

The book *Tiferes Banim* (Chapter 179) tells the following story:

> An inspector from a certain municipality came to claim municipal taxes from me. When I told him that I'd already paid, he said, "Show me the receipt." I told him, "Go check the municipality's accounting books and you'll see that I paid." A few days later, he came back to me and said that he'd looked and couldn't find it. He told me to pay the taxes right away. I insisted that I'd already paid and would not pay twice. He threatened that if I didn't pay immediately, he would take me to court. And that's what he did—he summoned me to court.
>
> When I came to court, the judge told me that I had to pay the taxes. I told him that I'd already paid. The judge said, "Where is the receipt?" I took the receipt out of my pocket and showed it to him. The judge asked me, "Why didn't you show this to the inspector when he came to claim the taxes from you?" I said to him, "I wanted to prove to you how completely disorganized they are."

A friend of mine told me a similar story. His son had to have a procedure in a certain hospital about twenty years ago. He paid on the spot with cash. Two years later, he received a warning from the hospital that he had not paid on time and also had to pay heavy fines. It was later discovered that the secretary had taken the money for herself and assumed that he lost his receipt.

My friend, however, was always very organized. He took the receipt out of the file and sent it to the hospital. The hospital canceled the claim and apologized. In the end, they caught the secretary and she was punished.

CHALLENGE FOR THE WEEK

This week, let's try to make sure that we make our beds each morning.

Being the First to Greet Everyone

The stairwell was dark. Dovid reached for the light switch and turned on the light. That's when he saw someone open the door on the first floor. It was Rabbi Cohen, his elderly neighbor who was about to go out.

Dovid ran up the stairs but it was too late. His neighbor had already seen him. "Shalom!" said Rabbi Cohen loudly.

Dovid's face went red. He was too embarrassed to answer. Rabbi Cohen was very well-known. In fact, he'd written quite a few sefarim on halachah. Many people would come to discuss different issues with him and ask him for advice, but Dovid was shy. Somehow, though, Rabbi Cohen always managed to bump into him and say hello. Dovid didn't know what to say when this happened.

Maybe he could try and sneak up the stairs and run into his home? Then he wouldn't have to deal with it.

Rabbi Cohen didn't let him, though. "Where are you going, my young friend?" he asked with a smile. Dovid realized that he had no choice but to go back down the stairs and say hello.

"Why don't you answer?" Rabbi Cohen asked gently. *"I said hello to you."*

"Hello," whispered Dovid shyly. From the smile on Rabbi Cohen's face, Dovid saw that Rabbi Cohen really appreciated his greeting. Even if it was from a little boy who happened to be one of his neighbors in the building.

QUESTIONS FOR THE FAMILY

- Do you usually say hello to other people?
- Should a person greet every person he or she meets?
- Do you respond to people who greet you?

In this week's *parashah*, it says: " יברכך ה' וישמרך. יאר ה' פניו אליך ויחונך. ישא ה' פניו אליך וישם לך שלום.—May Hashem bless you and protect you. May He make His presence enlighten you and have compassion on you. May Hashem turn His attention to you and grant you **peace**" (*Bamidbar* 6:24).

Chazal (*Berachos* 6b) said that it is important to be the first to greet a person, as it says: "Seek peace and pursue it." And if a person was greeted and didn't greet back, then he's called a thief.

We learn from here that greeting someone is a *middah tovah*. Also, the opposite is true: not greeting someone back is regarded as a serious *aveirah*.

Here is a great question to think about. Why does a person say *"Shalom Aleichem"* when he meets a friend but when the friend answers, he switches the order and says, *"Aleichem Shalom"*?

The great Rabbi Moshe Shapira, *zt"l*, answers this, based on the Gemara (*Nedarim* 10a). Let's say that a person decides to give an offering

to Hashem. He should not say: "עולה לה'" (to Hashem I will give an elevation-offering). This is because the person may die right after saying Hashem's name, and then he would have said Hashem's name in vain. Instead, he should switch the words around and say: "עולה לה'" (I will give an elevation-offering to Hashem). But this is difficult. Because if this is true, then how can a person say, "*Shalom Aleichem*?" He's saying the word "*Shalom*" first and this is the name of Hashem!

The answer is based on what Chazal said: "Whoever greets his friend first lives longer." This means that the person who greets his friend first doesn't have to worry that he will die at that moment because he is guaranteed to live a long life, so he can say "*Shalom Aleichem*." His friend, though, who didn't greet him first, does not have that guarantee. That's why he has to say, "*Aleichem Shalom*."

"It is said about Rabbi Yochanan ben Zakai that he was always the first to greet other people, even the non-Jew in the marketplace" (*Berachos* 17a). He did this because every person is created in the image of Hashem and deserves to be appreciated and greeted.

There is a story about the great Rabbi Shmuel Shapira, zt"l, who was the highly-respected rabbi of the Polish city called Pronkik. Rabbi Shapira would often go for a walk to make sure that he stayed healthy. He was liked by everyone and would greet every person he met, even non-Jews.

One of the people that he often met on his walks and greeted was a Polish farmer by the name of Miller. When the Rabbi first met and greeted Mr. Miller, the farmer would turn away and not even answer. This was because the Jews and non-Jews in that city didn't get on so well with each other.

But Rabbi Shapira did not give up. Day after day, he would greet the unfriendly Mr. Miller with a warm "Hello, Sir Miller." Eventually Mr. Miller softened up slightly. He even responded to the Rabbi's greeting by lifting his hat and giving a faint smile. This routine continued for years.

Until the Nazis came. Rabbi Shapira and his family, together with all the Jewish residents of the city, were sent to the concentration camps.

One day, Rabbi Shapira arrived at Auschwitz. He got off the train and was told to join the line in which the "selection" was taking place (this meant that it was being decided who would live and who wouldn't). His heart was pounding with fear. He moved forward; it was about to be his turn. What would his verdict be? Would it be toward the left and to death? Or toward the right and to life?

Even though he was extremely scared, Rabbi Shapira looked directly at the Nazi officer. Their eyes met. Rabbi Shapira recognized him. He leaned forward and whispered, "Good morning, Herr (German for 'Sir') Miller!" Miller's cold, impenetrable eyes flinched for a fraction of a second. "Good morning, Herr Rabbiner (German for 'Sir Rabbi')," he muttered back, and told him to go to the right (which meant life).

CHALLENGE FOR THE WEEK

This week, let's try to say hello to people *before* they greet us.

Dealing with the Sneaky Yetzer Hara

Dovid filled up his cup with water, made a berachah, and began to drink. A second later, he spat out the water into the sink. "Gross! This water tastes terrible!" he said, disgusted.

"Dovid! You should know it's not nice to spit like that!" said his sister.

"But the water tastes disgusting!" explained Dovid. "Maybe there's something wrong with the tap."

"No, the tap's fine!" she said. Just to make sure, she took a cup and filled it up from the tap. She made a berachah and took a small sip. "Nothing wrong. Tastes okay to me!" she said.

"That's weird," said Dovid and filled his cup again. He took a big sip and almost choked. "Yuck! Disgusting!"

Their mother came to see what was going on. She listened carefully as Dovid complained that his water had a strange taste. "Can you show me your cup please?" she asked.

Dovid gave the cup to his mother. She took one look at it and

knew exactly what had happened. "Tell me," she said to Dovid, "what did you do after you finished drinking your chocolate milk this morning?"

"What'd I do this morning?" Dovid repeated. He tried to remember...He had drunk the chocolate milk, said borei nefashos, and was about to leave the kitchen when his mother had stopped him and said, "Just a second, Dovid! Please wash your cup first." But he didn't have time. "I'm in a rush!" he said and ran out of the kitchen. It was true. He had to go and memorize mishnayos by heart. His rebbi had said that today he was going to test those boys who had managed to learn all the mishnayos. So Dovid wanted to go prepare so that he could do really well.

Now Dovid understood why the water tasted so bad. It wasn't the water after all. It was the cup. He'd used the same cup that still had some chocolate milk in it from this morning. That explained why the water was so bad!

Dovid thought about everything that happened. His mother had asked him to wash the cup. The truth is that he didn't feel like doing it. Instead, he decided to do a different mitzvah—to go learn mishnayos. He lost out on the first mitzvah because he wanted to do a different mitzvah. That didn't really make sense! Dovid realized that the yetzer hara had tricked him. "Next time, I'd better stop and think. Then I can make the best decision," he said to himself.

QUESTIONS FOR THE FAMILY

- Has it ever happened that you do a mitzvah to get out of doing a different mitzvah?
- Do you also sometimes get confused about if something is a mitzvah or not?

It says in the *haftarah* that we read this Shabbos: "And the Satan was standing on his right side in order to accuse him" (*Zechariah* 3:1).

The Chafetz Chaim, *zt"l*, in his commentary on Chumash (*Parashas Beha'alosecha*) asked: "Why does the Satan stand on the *right-hand* side? Isn't his place always on the left? Usually, the right represents good while the left means bad, so the prosecutor should always be on the left side!

He answered that when the Satan wants to trick people, he uses the right-hand side. He makes them think that they are doing mitzvos when they are actually doing *aveiros*. To help us understand this idea, the Chafetz Chaim gives the following example. The *yetzer hara* can convince a person to wake up early and run to shul, but it could be that the person is excited to go to shul for the wrong reason. The *yetzer hara* may know that this person will talk in shul during davening or Torah reading, or that he will speak *lashon hara* with his friends.

Remember that the *yetzer hara* sometimes comes to you in disguise. He may pretend to be the *yetzer hatov*, and give you all sorts of excuses why you shouldn't do what you're supposed to do. For example, instead of washing the dishes, the *yetzer hara* may try to convince you that you need to take a break or do a different "mitzvah."

There was once a Jew who brought home a large chunk of meat. He roasted it and ate some of it for supper. He saved the rest for later. Later that week, his wife reheated the meat and they had some more of it. A few days after that, she took the leftover meat out of the fridge. "What are you going to do with that?" the husband asked. "Throw it in the trash," said his wife, "the meat probably isn't good anymore."

"You're doing an *aveirah*. The Torah says that we shouldn't waste food!" the man told his wife. He took the meat from his wife and put it on the table. Just then, he looked outside the window and saw his neighbor. The man called out to his neighbor. "Look, I bought a lot of meat and there's still some left. Would you like it?" he said. The neighbor's eyes lit up and he took the meat very happily and went home. "You see," the husband said to his wife, "we almost missed out on a mitzvah!"

The next day, the couple heard that their neighbor had gotten very sick from food poisoning. The man quickly ran over to his neighbor to do the mitzvah of visiting the sick. Unfortunately, the neighbor got worse and passed away. When the man heard about his neighbor's death, he went to the funeral, followed slowly behind the coffin, and walked all the way to the grave. Afterward, he went to do the mitzvah of comforting the mourners.

When he came home, he said to his wife, "You see, this is what the Rabbis said, 'One mitzvah leads to another mitzvah!' First, we did a *chessed* by giving the meat. After that, we did the mitzvah of visiting the sick, then accompanying the dead, and now comforting the mourners. And if you would've thrown the meat in the trash, you would've prevented us from doing all these mitzvos!"

From this, we can see how much the *yetzer hara* can truly confuse people!

CHALLENGE FOR THE WEEK

After a meal, let's help right away by clearing our plates and cutlery, and putting them in the sink.

PARASHAS SHELACH

Seeing Things Positively

The store in his neighborhood was having a sale on balls. How did Dovid know? Simple. His grandmother had come to visit yesterday. On her way, she had stopped at the store and bought him a ball for a present. When he brought the ball to class today, he discovered that Yehudah had the exact same ball.

"Where's the ball from?" Dovid asked.

"My aunt bought it for me," said Yehudah cheerfully. "It's a neat ball, right?"

Not really, thought Dovid. If just Dovid had the ball, then it would have been neat. But because Yehudah also had a new ball, all the friends weren't so excited about Dovid's ball.

"This is a really cool ball!" shouted Yehudah excitedly. "Did you see? It bounces so well!"

Dovid bounced his ball. Yes, it did bounce quite well. After two minutes, though, he already wasn't so excited about the way that it bounced.

They were playing in the playground and Yossi threw the ball. The ball went flying and landed in the bushes behind the fence.

"Oh no!" said Dovid angrily. "What a stupid ball!"

At the same time, Yehudah was playing with his friends on the other side of the playground. He threw the ball to Gadi who stuck out his foot and kicked the ball. The ball spun in the air and landed on top of the tree nearby.

"Cool!" shouted Yehudah. "Let's go and see who can get the ball down!"

At the end of recess, both boys came back with their balls. But they definitely had different attitudes.

"Whew!" complained Dovid. "By the time we got the ball out of the bushes, almost the whole recess was over. What a stupid ball! And what a waste of time."

"That was great!" smiled Yehudah. "Boy, did we work hard to get the ball down. Recess was really fun today!"

QUESTIONS FOR THE FAMILY

- Why are some people positive while others are negative?
- Do you usually complain or do you see the good?

Rabbeinu Yonah (*Shaarei Teshuvah*, end of the third *shaar*) calls a person who views everything negatively a *nargan*. This type of person is always moaning about something. He keeps on telling people that he's losing out and being picked on. He complains the whole time and thinks that everybody's out to get him.

Rabbeinu Yonah says that this person also complains about Hashem. Even when Hashem does something good for him, he finds a way to show that it's actually bad for him. *Narganim* are experts at finding faults in other people and think that whatever happens is bad. They

never see what's really happening to them and always find a way to twist things around.

The Torah tells us that it was this bad *middah* that made the Spies do what they did. After all the times that Hashem showed his kindness to the Jewish People when He took them out of Egypt, the Jews sat in their tents and complained. They found ways to explain that all the good things that Hashem had done for them were bad. One time, they even said: "Hashem hates us and took us out of Egypt to hand us over to the Emori so that He could wipe us out."

The Gemara in *Sotah* (35a) tells us that Rava taught: "Hashem said, 'I meant it for good but they saw it as bad.'" The Gemara explains that Hashem made some of the local people die so that their people would be too busy burying them and not notice the Spies, but the Spies interpreted this as a bad thing. They said that the land was so bad that it made the people die.

Also, when the Spies came back with the bad report, the Torah says that the Jewish People cried. The Gemara, however, tells us the *real* reason why they cried. It was really because of the Spies' *ayin ra'ah* toward Eretz Yisrael. This made them come and complain instead of being grateful to Hashem for doing so many incredible miracles to save them. This shows how being negative affected the way the Jews looked at things.

There is a story about four blind people who were standing together. All of a sudden, someone told them that there was an elephant trainer with an elephant coming toward them.

"What does an elephant look like?" asked the blind people curiously. They asked the elephant trainer if they could touch the elephant to feel what it was like.

Each of the blind people touched a different part of the elephant. The first one touched the trunk, the second touched the foot, the third touched the stomach, and the fourth touched the tail.

Then the elephant trainer asked them, "Now do you know what an elephant is like?" "Sure" the blind people answered.

"So, what exactly is an elephant like?" he asked.

Each of them gave a different answer. "It's like a snake that's twisted into a ring," said the blind person who had touched the trunk.

"You're wrong," shouted the blind person who had touched the elephant's foot. "It's not like a snake. It's like a round stone pillar."

"No, it's like a gigantic barrel of water," declared the third blind person, who had touched the elephant's stomach.

"You're all wrong," said the fourth blind person, who had touched its tail. "An elephant is like the thick rope of a ship."

They didn't understand that the only thing that is like an elephant is…an elephant.

It's true that there are some bad things in the world, but we also need to know that there are lots of good things. Our job is to learn how to look at things properly and positively. In general, things are usually pretty good!

CHALLENGE FOR THE WEEK

When we come home each day, let's try to tell everybody about something good that happened to us during the day.

Being Truly Happy

Dovid was lost in his thoughts as he walked home with his father from Maariv. Dovid's father was surprised and very curious. He wasn't used to seeing his son walking quietly, without running or jumping. "What happened? What are you thinking about?" he asked Dovid.

"About Gadi," answered Dovid as he looked up.

"Gadi? From your class?"

"Yeah. Abba, his family is so rich!" All of a sudden, Dovid was full of energy. He walked with more spring in his step, the way he normally walked. "They have a two-story house, a huge garden with lots of plants, and special chairs and benches. One time, I went to get a notebook from him—what a fancy house! As you walk in, it has this type of carpet, in a red-and-white color. And the walls are full of pictures. And they have a giant decoration made from a mirror at the entrance...they're so lucky!"

"Really?" asked his father.

"What do you mean 'really'?" asked Dovid, a little confused.

"Is it really so wonderful for them? They're always so happy because they have a lot of money?" asked his father.

Dovid thought for a moment. "Not all the time," he admitted. "His baby sister was in the hospital for a long time and they weren't happy then."

"You see," said his father. "Money doesn't always bring happiness, right? In fact, rich people aren't the only ones who can be happy. Anyone who uses his money to do mitzvos can be happy. That's because true happiness comes from doing a mitzvah. What do you think, Dovid?"

Dovid smiled. "Today, I was very happy," he told his father. "I talked with a boy, whose name I don't want to tell, because it would be lashon hara. He's a boy nobody pays attention to in class. But today, I went up to him and talked a little with him, and then he started smiling and looked happy. And that's when I felt happy too!"

QUESTIONS FOR THE FAMILY

- Do you feel happy?
- What makes you feel happy?

When people want to describe a very wealthy person in Hebrew, they often use the expression, "As rich as Korach." Chazal (*Pesachim* 119a) say that Korach found one of the treasure houses that Yosef had hidden in Egypt. It was so full of treasure that three hundred donkeys were needed just to carry the *keys* to Korach's treasure houses!

But there were many incredibly wealthy people in the world; why is *Korach* specifically used as the example of a very rich person?

The answer is that even though Korach was extremely wealthy, he didn't use his wealth properly. The Torah describes how Korach and all his possessions were swallowed up by the ground. This shows us that a person should only use his money and possessions for good things. And that's why Korach is used as the example. When people say, "As rich as Korach," this reminds us what happens when wealth isn't used properly.

There is a *pasuk* in *Koheles* (5:12) that says that if a person keeps all his wealth to himself, he will lose out. Chazal (*Midrash Rabbah*) explain that this is talking about Korach. He used his wealth for bad things and in the end, he and everything that he had disappeared into the ground.

A story is told in *Tuvecha Yabiyu* (volume 2, page 309) about a very poor woman who once knocked on the door of a *talmid chacham*, a very well-known person in Yerushalayim. She begged him to give her some meat or chicken for *yom tov*. The man himself earned a small salary and gave what he could to *ma'aser* and *tzedakah*. He tried to explain to the woman that he only had two chickens and he was saving them for his own family for *yom tov*. The woman remained at the door and begged the man to give her food so that she wouldn't die from hunger.

The man listened and thought about the situation. He said to himself, "If this poor woman isn't embarrassed to come to my door and ask for food, then she really must be desperate. If that's true, then maybe I should give her some chicken." He knew that he also had very little, but he was always happy with whatever he had.

He quickly apologized to her and asked her to wait while he went to get the chicken from the fridge.

The man went to the fridge, opened it...and let out a scream.

As he opened the fridge, he saw a small child stuck inside. It was his three-year-old son who had gotten locked in the fridge. During a game of hide-and-seek, he had climbed into the fridge and couldn't open the door from the inside.

The child could hardly breathe and was already blue. Miraculously, the paramedics were able to get him to breathe normally again. According to the details of the medical report, if the child would've stayed in the fridge even a little bit longer, he wouldn't have been alive.

This person was happy with the little that he had, and that's why he was prepared to share and give to the poor person. From this, we see that a person doesn't lose out from doing mitzvos. He gave a quarter of a chicken and received an entire child instead. Even though the man was happy before, now he had even more reason to be happy. Doing mitzvos, especially giving to other people, brings true happiness.

CHALLENGE FOR THE WEEK

This week, let's try to do things that will make us feel truly happy.

PARASHAS CHUKAS

Measure for Measure

Dovid came back from shul on Friday night with bulging pock-ets. The gabbai had given out lollipops to all the children who had put the siddurim back on the bookshelf. Dovid had put back five siddurim and got two lollipops. Then Rabbi Levy handed out toffees to all the children. And Dovid made sure to get seven of those too. On their way home, they met Uncle Chaim, who also gave him six sourballs.

At home, Dovid took out his treasures and laid them out on the table. Wow! Toffees, sourballs, and two lollipops. So exciting!

Right then his sister walked past. He quickly grabbed all the candies and put them back in his pocket. But she had already seen. "Where did you get so many candies?" she asked.

"From shul," he answered and put his hand over his pocket to make sure that she couldn't grab anything. "You already got a candy at kabbalas Shabbos."

Dovid knew, though, that her candy had already been eaten long ago. And he still had so many left.

She didn't say anything but Dovid could see that she was

staring at the pocket where the candies were. She really did want a candy.

He took out a sourball from his pocket. "Do you want?" he asked. She said, "Yes, please!" She took it and ran away, very excited.

The next morning, there was a chassan in shul. The women threw lots of packets of candy at the end of krias haTorah. Even though Dovid really tried, he didn't manage to grab even one packet of candy. Out of the corner of his eye, he noticed that his friends were each holding two or three packets. He was the only one who didn't get anything.

Right then, Moishie walked past him and realized what happened. "Do you want?" he asked—just like Dovid had asked his sister yesterday—and offered him two packets of candy filled with all sorts of goodies.

QUESTIONS FOR THE FAMILY

- The story describes a way that Hashem conducts the world: *middah k'neged middah*—measure for measure. Where do we see this type of conduct being expressed in the story?
- Can you give an example where you behaved in a certain way (good or bad) and afterward you noticed that Hashem behaved toward you in a similar way?

It says in the *parashah*: "And Hashem punished the people with poisonous snakes and they bit the people and many Jews died" (*Bamidbar* 21:6).

Why did Hashem punish the nation specifically with snakes?

Rashi quotes the *Midrash Tanchuma* and explains that the reason is measure for measure. Let the snake, which was punished for speaking

negatively about its Creator, come and punish the Jewish People for speaking negatively about the *mann*. Let the snake, for whom everything that it eats has one taste, namely sand, come and punish those who were ungrateful, having bad-mouthed the *mann*, which would change into different flavors for them.

The *Kli Yakar* adds that the snake, which sinned with speech, attacks those who speak hurtful words. This is the reason why they were commanded to look at the snake and thereby be healed. When they looked at the snake, they would remember what happened to the original snake because of his words. They would then regret that they spoke negatively and resolve to repent fully.

This practice of measure for measure also applies nowadays in a very clear way. The Rambam explains the following Mishnah in *Pirkei Avos* (2:7) as a clear demonstration of how Hashem runs the world with *Hashgachah pratis*. The Mishnah says that Hillel saw a skull that was floating on the surface of the water. He said to it, "You were drowned because you drowned (others), and eventually the people who drowned you will be drowned." In other words: "You were killed because you killed others, and whoever killed you will eventually be killed." This means that people who do bad things are punished so that those bad things happen to them, like it says: "The wicked person will be trapped by his own sins..." (*Mishlei* 5:22) and "He dug a deep pit and will fall into a trap that he himself made" (*Tehillim* 7:16). Chazal (*Sotah* 8b) said: "A person is treated in the same way that he treats others."

There is a story about a beggar who hadn't had anything to eat on *erev Yom Kippur*. He decided that if he couldn't have anything to eat, he would at least try to get a whiff of snuff. He went up to one of the wealthy people in shul and told him what he wanted. At that moment, the wealthy person was busy saying *vidui*, and refused to interrupt his davening to give some snuff to the beggar.

When the Heavenly court saw this, a huge uproar arose. How could a Jew could refuse to give snuff to a Jew who hadn't eaten the entire day?! It was decreed that wealthy person and the beggar would switch positions. And that's what happened—the beggar became rich and the wealthy person became poor. The person who used to be wealthy became very sad about his fate and went to consult the rabbi about his bad fortune.

After asking a few questions, the rabbi realized what had happened. He said to the person who used to be wealthy, "You should know that you brought about your own punishment by refusing to give a little snuff to that beggar who hadn't eaten the entire day." When the wealthy person asked how he could fix the situation, the rabbi said, "If you find yourself in the original situation, in the reversed way, where you come to him and ask him for snuff and he refuses, the situation will return to how it was originally." The formerly wealthy person looked for the right moment and, lo and behold, he found the appropriate opportunity to do it.

It was on a day that the former beggar was extremely busy—the day of his daughter's wedding. At this time, when the former beggar was very busy taking care of his guests, the formerly wealthy person went up to him and pleaded with him, "Sir, please could you give me a pinch of snuff to smell?" When the father of the bride heard this, he quickly took the silver container of snuff out of his pocket and offered the man graciously: "Please take as much as you want." The formerly wealthy person fainted on the spot. After they revived him and asked him to tell them what had happened to him, he told them about everything that occurred to him as well as the rabbi's advice. From that day onward, the formerly wealthy person ate his meals at the home of the the former beggar, who took care of all his needs.

CHALLENGE FOR THE WEEK

This week, let's try to do a favor for a friend. Then we can be sure that the Heavenly court will also judge us in the same way: measure for measure.

Learning Torah with Excitement

Dovid's mother noticed the envelope right away. She was already familiar with the envelopes that had the school logo. She knew them all too well; Dovid had brought home quite a few of these envelopes recently. Each time, the envelope had some type of note inside that had not such good news:

"Dovid doesn't always manage to behave as he should."

"Sometimes Dovid gets mixed up and forgets how to speak to a teacher."

"This is not the first time that Dovid has gotten into an argument with a friend where the argument went a little too far."

And now, once again, Dovid walked in holding an envelope.

His mother sighed quietly. What a pity that Dovid didn't control himself as much as he should. Surprisingly, Dovid didn't look like he usually did when he was holding an envelope from school. His eyes shone and had a sparkle in them. His mother had not seen his face look like this for a long time.

"Did Abba already come back?" Dovid asked.

"Yes," said Dovid's father as he walked into the kitchen. He also noticed the envelope right away. "How're you doing, Dovid? What's going on?"

Dovid handed him the envelope with a proud look on his face. "It's from my rebbi," he said, without giving a clue what it was about.

His father slowly opened the seal and took out the school letter. It looked exactly like the other ones. But this time the message was very different.

Dovid's father read it. Then he read it again. And after the third time, he looked up. His eyes were shining too—just like Dovid's.

"Imma," he said with a broad smile, "I would like to read to you what the rebbi wrote:"

> To the parents of my dear student Dovid,
>
> Dovid learned today with tremendous enthusiasm. You can be very proud of your son. May he continue to grow in his love for learning!

Now Dovid's mother's eyes also shone. They all looked at each other with huge smiles on their faces. They took the letter and read the line again: "May he continue to grow in his love for learning!"

QUESTION FOR THE FAMILY

Do you also try to learn Torah with excitement?

It says in this week's *parashah*: "Hashem took them out of Egypt; like the incredible strength of a *re'eim* [a type of giant wild-ox] which He has" (*Bamidbar* 23:22).

The Gemara (*Gittin* 68b) points out that it was forbidden to use metal objects to build the Beis Hamikdash. This is what it says in *Melachim I* (6:7): "And when the Beis Hamikdash was built, it was constructed from whole, quarried stone." As a result, Shlomo HaMelech asked the sages how he could make sure that the stone would be smooth and chiseled, without using metal. The sages told him that that he could use the *shamir* worm that Moshe Rabbeinu had used to cut the precious stones of the breastplate. Shlomo asked them where he could find this *shamir* and they replied: "Take a male demon and a female demon, force both of them and they will tell you." After he did that, they told him that they didn't know but that Ashmedai, the king of the evil spirits, would know.

"Where can he be found?" Shlomo asked them. They told him that he could be found on a certain mountain and they taught him how to catch him. They explained that Ashmedai comes down to earth every day and drinks water from a certain well. Shlomo replaced the well's water with wine. When Ashmedai drank, he fell asleep and then Shlomo tied him up with a chain on which the name of Hashem was engraved. Since the Heavenly name was written on it and it was forbidden to destroy it, Ashmedai would not be able to break the chain.

When they brought Ashmedai to Shlomo, Ashmedai told him that he did not have the *shamir* but the angel of the sea did and he would occasionally give it to the wild rooster to use on a temporary basis. Shlomo covered the bird's nest with a transparent glass. When the rooster was not able to get in, it flew away to bring the *shamir*. When it came to the nest, Shlomo's agent threw a clod of earth at it and took the *shamir*. That's how Shlomo cut the stones of the Beis Hamikdash.

One day, Shlomo asked Ashmedai, "Please explain to me the following. It says in the Torah: 'Like the incredible strength of a *re'eim* [a type of giant wild-ox] which He has.'" This *pasuk* implies that demons are more powerful than people. "Please tell me: In what way are you so powerful that the *pasuk* should hold you in such high esteem?" Ashmedai said to him, "Remove the chain and I will show you how powerful I am." Shlomo released him and then Ashmedai gave him such a strong whack with his wing that Shlomo flew a distance of four hundred *parsahs* (approximately 1,000 miles or 1,600 km)! It took a long time until Shlomo was able to resume his position as king...

This is difficult to understand. How could Shlomo HaMelech, the wisest of all people, unchain Ashmedai? How did he not consider that the demon would probably harm him?

This issue can be explained as follows. Shlomo HaMelech lived by the *pasuk* (*Mishlei* 5:19): "You will always be madly in love with her (i.e., the Torah)!" This means that he so desperately wanted to know the meaning of the phrase: "Like the incredible strength of a *re'eim* [a type of giant wild-ox] which He has," that he was prepared to risk being harmed! That's how much he loved Torah!

CHALLENGE FOR THE WEEK

Let's try to learn Torah with lots of excitement and enthusiasm.

Being Extra Kind to Others

"Dovid," his mother asked one Thursday night. "Please tidy your room, put away the chairs, and take the scooter out to the balcony."

"Okay," Dovid said, and he went and did it. He collected the crayons that were all over the floor, threw the used pages in the trash, and put the books back on the shelf. He put the chairs away and took the scooter to the balcony.

He was about to go and tell his mother that he had finished. But then he had an idea.

He thought about what his mother had asked him to do. Why did she ask him to tidy his room? And why did she want him to move the chairs?

Obviously, she wanted to clean the floor for Shabbos.

Well, then, he would help some more. He decided that he would go and sweep it himself. It was true that his mother hadn't asked him to sweep. She'd only said that he should move the items that were on the floor. But he knew why she'd asked him to do it. So why not help a little more? If he swept, then all she needed to do was mop the floor.

Dovid took the broom and swept the whole room. Then he went to tell his mother that he had finished.

She thanked him and then peeked inside. "What? You also swept?" she said with excitement. "Even though I didn't ask? That's so beautiful! This shows how kind you are!"

QUESTION FOR THE FAMILY
Do you also try to do more than you were asked?

It says in the *parashah* that Moshe Rabbeinu put his hands on Yehoshua (*Bamidbar* 27:23). Rashi says: "With tremendous kindness—much more than he was told to. Even though Hashem had told him: 'Put your *hand*,' he did it with *both* of his hands. By doing this, Moshe gave so much wisdom to Yehoshua that he was like a container that was overflowing."

The *Ba'alei HaTosfos* (*Bava Kamma* 92b) compare this to a master who tells his servant to give wine to his friend. The servant went and gave a top-quality wine to his master's friend.

The master was very happy because the servant had done more than he was told to. This is what happened when Hashem told Moshe, "Put your *hand* on him" and he put *both* hands.

The *sefer He'oros B'Avodas Hashem* says that a person should train himself to want to help others. That's why he should try not to be stingy. In fact, he should give even more to others than he would to himself, because that's what he would want others to do for him. He should try to be kind to everybody. For example, when he buys an item, he should try to pay the seller a little more than what it's worth. This will make

the seller feel good. Doing this develops the *middah* of being good and doing good.

The story is told in *Peninei Mishmar HaLevi* (volume 3) of Rabbi Shlomo Cohen, who was one of the first people to live in B'nei Brak. He started a printing business there and worked hard to take care of his family. In the beginning, there weren't any other businesses in that area that did printing. His customers came from all over and his business became very successful. One day, another person came and opened a printing business not far away from Rabbi Cohen's business. Rabbi Cohen's children were very angry at this man who had the chutzpah to open the exact same business so close by. Their father, on the other hand, didn't get angry like them. In fact, he even went and welcomed the owner of the new printing press. Rabbi Cohen was very friendly and said to him, "I know that you're new to the area and probably don't have any customers yet. Come, I'll give you a list of customers." On the spot, he gave him a long list of his own customers. Rabbi Cohen told him that he was very happy to let him do business with them, but he didn't stop there. He also said to him, "Come, I'll teach you how to do the work even better so that everybody will be happy with the jobs that you do for them."

This story teaches us to help other people even if we aren't asked. A giving person wants the best for the other person. And that's why he does more than he is asked to do.

CHALLENGE FOR THE WEEK

This week, let's try to be extra kind and do or give more than we're asked to.

Showing Appreciation

What a boiling hot day!

Dovid went to the fridge for the third time in an hour—another glass of cold water wouldn't hurt right now.

He took out the bottle of water, poured a glass for himself, made a berachah, and drank. After he finished saying borei nefashos, he was about to put the bottle back in the fridge. But then he stopped and thought for a second.

Right now, his mother was standing on the balcony in the boiling hot sun. She was busy hanging up laundry. If he was in the house and felt hot, then it must be very hot for her outside. That's when he had an idea. Maybe he should get a glass of cold water for his mother?

Dovid knew that this would take some effort. First, he would have to take a clean glass down from the shelf. Then fill it with water. And then carefully carry the full glass all the way to the balcony. His mother deserved it, though. In fact, she deserved so much more. After all, she was the one who got up early every morning to wake him up on time. She was the one who put clean, folded clothes next to the bed for him every night. She was the one who cooked a hot, filling meal for him every day. And she was the one who loved him, davened for his success, and did so many other things for him.

He decided that he should make a little effort to do something. Even if it was something small, it was for his mother, who always did so much for him. This was besides for the mitzvah to honor parents.

Dovid filled a glass with cold water and walked carefully to the balcony. Just then, his mother reached down into the huge laundry basket and took out a familiar-looking pair of pants—his pants. She stood up and was about to hang up the pants when she saw her precious son with a cup of cold water in his hand.

"Thank you, Dovid!" The twinkle that sparkled in his mother's eyes was worth more to him than anything else.

QUESTIONS FOR THE FAMILY

- What do you think a person should be grateful for?
- How is it possible to show appreciation?

In this week's *parashah* Hashem says to Moshe: "Take revenge for B'nei Yisrael against the people of Midyan; after which you will be gathered to your people [i.e. pass away]" (*Bamidbar* 31:2).

Moshe Rabbeinu was told by Hashem to go fight with Midyan. He himself didn't fight, though; instead, he sent Pinchas to be in charge of the army. Why? Because Moshe was grateful to the people of Midyan for helping him when he ran away from Egypt. The *Midrash* (*Bamidbar Rabbah* 22:4) says: "Do not throw a stone into a well from which you

drank." So even though the Jews had to attack Midyan, *Moshe* didn't want to be the one to do so.

Rabbi Pinchas Segel was a child during the Holocaust. He survived by being hidden by a priest. One day, the priest threatened him that if he didn't convert to Christianity, then he wouldn't be allowed to continue hiding by him, so he decided to run away. He found a temporary shelter and knocked on the door, hoping that they would give him some food. Unfortunately, this was the home of a Nazi officer, who noticed right away that he was Jewish. He grabbed the boy and started interrogating him. "How did you manage until now? Who hid you away?" the Nazi shouted. Pinchas didn't want to tell him because he was very grateful to the priest. The Nazi beat him up quite badly but Pinchas still refused to say who had helped him. Even though the priest had been prepared to kick him out of the house, Pinchas chose to get hurt rather than let the priest be killed. He was grateful to the priest for hiding him away for such a long time.

CHALLENGE FOR THE WEEK
This week, let's try to show appreciation to someone specific.

Not Pushing Others

What's going on here?! He'd already been waiting at the bus stop for twenty minutes and the bus still hadn't arrived. Chaim looked at the huge crowd at the bus stop. Everyone was waiting for the same bus, and more people were arriving as each minute went by. "When the bus does eventually get here, it's going to be completely full!" said Chaim to himself.

One person called the information hotline for public transportation. It said that the bus was on the way and would be there in one or two minutes. But it seemed that the bus didn't get that message. Another five minutes went by and it still hadn't shown up.

Everybody was becoming impatient. Some complained about how bad the bus company was. Others suggested that someone should send them a letter of complaint. Some just said that this type of delay was unacceptable.

Then the bus arrived.

The front door was definitely not wide enough for such a huge crowd. In a second, a long, loud queue was standing at the door.

Chaim knew that he didn't stand a chance of getting on. There were lots of people in front of him and the bus was already quite full. The driver would probably close the doors even before he could get on…

There was one way to get on, though—to push. He could jump into the crowd, push and be pushed, and then maybe he would be able to get on the bus.

Was it worth it?

QUESTIONS FOR THE FAMILY

- Do you also push to get on the bus?
- What should Chaim do in this situation?

In the *parashah*, it says: "And all of you came to me" (*Devarim* 1:22). Rashi explains: "In chaos. Children pushing old people, and old people pushing the leaders." Everyone crowded around Moshe without any *derech eretz*.

Hashem warned about this problem earlier on. By the building and carrying of the *Mishkan*, it says: "And Hashem spoke to Moshe and Aharon saying, 'Don't let the tribal families of Kehas be cut off from the rest of the *Levi'im*'" (*Bamidbar* 4:18). Rashi explains that this means to make sure that they don't die.

The *Sforno* explains that this means that the rule shouldn't be that whoever gets to the *klei haMikdash* first gets to carry them. This might lead to people pushing each other. And this would be a disgrace to the *Aron haKodesh*. This would result in them "being cut off," which is spiritual death. By doing this, they would do a double *aveirah: bein adam l'chaveiro* and *bein adam laMakom*.

The Mishnah (*Yoma* 2:1–2) says:

In the beginning, whoever wanted to clear the ashes from the Mizbei'ach could go and do it. When a few people wanted to do it, they would have a race up the ramp. Whoever got to the top first won the right to do the job. One time, two people were running up the ramp and were exactly equal, but then one of them pushed his friend and he broke his leg. When beis din saw that this approach was dangerous, they decided to use a lottery instead.

CHALLENGE FOR THE WEEK

Let's try to behave with *derech eretz* and not push to go into a room, onto a bus, or into an elevator.

Giving Nachas

Every week, Chaim put in a lot of effort to prepare a dvar Torah to say at the Shabbos table.

It wasn't at all simple.

Firstly, he had to find the time. This meant giving up on riding his bike or playing a game of tag with friends in the yard. Instead of playing, he had to sit down and prepare at home or in shul.

The second challenge was to find the right sefer. Sometimes Ma'ayanah shel Torah had an amazing idea but they didn't have this set at home. So he had to go to shul, remember to take a pen and paper, and read through the sefer until he found the right idea. At home, there were other sefarim, but those were very difficult for him to understand.

And this was the third problem: understanding the explanation. Chaim would read it over again and again until he understood it properly. He needed to know it so well that he could explain it to everybody else.

The last part was the hardest part: saying the dvar Torah.

Chaim had to read out whatever he had prepared—in front of everyone. In front of his older brothers, brothers-in-law, and sometimes guests, like the bachurim from the nearby yeshiva. For somebody as shy as Chaim, it wasn't easy to get up and speak in front of so many people.

Even though it was quite a challenge, Chaim worked hard to prepare a nice vort every week. He also practiced saying it out loud. Why? Because he saw the nachas that Abba and Imma got. He saw how much pleasure they got from him each Shabbos, and this gave him the energy to keep going.

QUESTIONS FOR THE FAMILY

- Do you also usually give a *dvar Torah* at the Shabbos meal?
- What are other good ways to give *nachas*?

It says in the *parashah*: "Honor your father and your mother as Hashem, your G-d, commanded you, so that you will live a long life and so that it will be good for you on the land that Hashem, your G-d, gives you" (*Devarim* 5:16).

There is a mitzvah for a child to give pleasure and *nachas* to his father and mother because this is how he honors them. If parents ask a child to prepare a *dvar Torah* for Shabbos, he should try to find an interesting *dvar Torah* and not just prepare something to get it over and done with. Obviously, a child can prepare a *dvar Torah* even *before* his parents ask—this would be an incredible way to show them respect.

A person can give *nachas* to his parents in other ways too. For example, he can compliment his mother on the delicious food that she made.

A group of *yeshiva bachurim* once asked the great Rav Yechezkel Levinstein, *zt"l*, about what to work on during *bein ha'zmanim*. He told

them that they should make sure to eat their mothers' home-cooked meals. That way their mothers would feel happy.

One of the *gedolim* taught his grandchildren to say the weekly *parashah* **loud and clear** to their grandmother so that she would be able to hear and get *nachas*. He would also say his *divrei Torah* loudly and clearly so that she could hear and enjoy.

CHALLENGE FOR THE WEEK

Let's try to prepare an interesting *dvar Torah* and say it clearly next Shabbos.

PARASHAS EIKEV

Being Grateful to Hashem

The alarm clock buzzed loudly. Chaim opened his eyes. In the meantime, his brother switched it off and started getting dressed. Chaim sat up but didn't get out of bed. He didn't even wash his hands; he just stayed there sitting on the bed, mumbling something to himself.

"What's going on?" his brother asked in surprise. "Why aren't you getting up?"

Chaim didn't answer. He looked like he was in a different world, thinking about something else.

Their mother came in to see that everyone had gotten up. She was also surprised to see Chaim, who wasn't doing anything at such a busy time in the morning. "Chaim, what's going on?" she asked.

Chaim answered by opening his eyes and saying each word carefully and with a lot of thought: "Modeh ani l'fanecha, Melech chai v'kayam, she'hechezarta bi nishmasi b'chemlah, rabbah emunasecha!" ["I am grateful to You, the King Who lives and exists forever, because You have given my soul back to me with a lot of mercy; Your loyalty is so great."]

"Wow!" exclaimed his brother.

"Beautiful!" said their mother. "That's the way that a person should thank Hashem every morning!"

"Is that why you were sitting so quietly before?" wondered his brother. "What were you whispering?"

Chaim smiled shyly and bent down to wash his hands. "Nu, what did you say so quietly before?" nudged his brother.

Chaim blushed. "I was thinking of all the amazing things that Hashem gave me. That I'm healthy. That I have parents and a family. That I have a home. That I did well on my test yesterday. And whatever else I could remember. After that, I thanked Hashem aloud."

"Amazing!" said their mother, very impressed. "I wish that all of us would learn from you how to thank Hashem."

QUESTIONS FOR THE FAMILY

- Is it easy for you to concentrate on the meaning of *Modeh Ani* when you say it?
- What else would you thank Hashem for?

It says in the *parashah*: "And you will eat, and you will be satisfied, and you will thank Hashem, your G-d, for the wonderful land that He gave you" (*Devarim* 8:10).

A person must thank Hashem for all the goodness that Hashem has given him.

The *Midrash* (*Megillas Rus Rabbah* 6:1) says that David HaMelech would wake up every night at midnight throughout his whole life. Then he would thank Hashem for all the kindness that Hashem had done for him and the Jewish People. He also thanked Hashem for making sure that his ancestor Rus was received kindly by Boaz, and not cursed when she paid him a surprise visit.

The great *tzaddik* Rabbi Yechezkel Abramsky, *zt"l*, would often say, "Let's look at what you think about when you come to shul and what David HaMelech thought about when he entered the house of Hashem. You might think that you are doing Hakadosh Baruch Hu a favor, but David HaMelech (*Tehillim* 5:8) said: "ואני ברוב חסדך אבוא ביתך—And I will enter Your house due to *Your abundant kindness*." He meant, "Hashem, You are so kind to me by giving me the opportunity to come to shul."

Like all the other *tefillos* and *berachos*, *Modeh Ani* should also be said slowly. A person should try to think about everything he has received, and still gets, from Hashem, i.e., that his whole family is alive and well and all the other kindnesses that Hashem has given to him. When he feels how much Hakadosh Baruch Hu loves him, then he will want to thank Him.

The gaon Rabbi Gamliel Rabinovitch, *shlita*, said that he once davened for something that he needed. A great *gadol* saw him and asked him, "Do you usually daven?"

"Yes," he answered.

He asked him again, "Did you ever feel that your *tefillah* was answered?"

"Of course," he replied.

"Did you also remember to thank Hashem after you got what you wanted?"

"Yes," he answered.

"Tell me honestly—how much time did you spend davening for something and how much time did you spend *thanking* Hashem for answering your *tefillah*? If you asked and davened for a half an hour for something, now you have to spend a half an hour *thanking* Him for giving it to you."

CHALLENGE FOR THE WEEK

When you wake up in the morning, try to say *Modeh Ani* aloud and with *kavanah*.

PARASHAS RE'EH

Caring about Siblings

One morning, Chaim opened his eyes. It looked like he was in a brand-new room. Everywhere was decorated with colorful balloons and signs. He closed his eyes, a little confused, and said Modeh Ani carefully and properly. After that, he opened his eyes, washed his hands, and got up to find out what all the fuss was about.

On the main sign, written with a purple marker, were the words: To our dear Chaim. Under that, written with a red marker, were the words: Good luck! Lots of colorful balloons had been stuck all around the sign. There were several more colorful cardboard signs around the room. All of them wished Chaim good luck for the new school year.

Chaim smiled and looked again at the beautiful signs. Every person in the family would get special berachos for every special occasion. It could be a great grade, a major test, an annual class trip, and obviously a birthday. Brothers and sisters would write personal notes, their parents would buy a small treat, and everyone would celebrate the exciting event together.

In his drawer, Chaim had a whole collection of these berachos from various occasions. It was so much fun to look through them every now and again!

He liked to organize these surprises for his siblings too. He would write personal messages if anything special was going on. There was always something to say thank you for. It also wasn't too difficult to find something to wish good luck for.

Now Chaim could go to school and not have to worry. He knew that his whole family was davening for his success and celebrating the new start together with him.

QUESTIONS FOR THE FAMILY

- Do you do anything like this in your family?
- What would you like to do for your family?

This week's *parashah* always comes before Elul. In fact, the word "ראה" is an acronym for "ראש (חודש) אלול הגיע, Rosh (Chodesh) Elul has arrived."

The *Saba* of Kelm would often say that the first letters of "אלול" stand for "אהוב למטה ונחמד למעלה—beloved below and treasured above." This means that a person should behave in a way that finds favor in the eyes of Hashem and people. On a similar note, Rabbi Meir Chodosh would emphasize that the most important thing during the month of Elul is to make other people happy.

One day, a *yeshiva bachur* arrived at the Yeshiva of Kelm. He started walking up the stairs of the yeshiva when, all of a sudden, one *bachur* came and gave him a warm handshake. He told the new *bachur* that he was very happy to meet him. The new *bachur* thought that the one who greeted him obviously knew him from somewhere else. As the new *bachur* walked up the stairs, the same thing happened quite a few times.

That's when he realized that the whole yeshiva excelled in the mitzvah of "caring about others."

There is another story about a *yeshiva bachur* who came to the yeshiva of Rabbi Chaim Shmulevitz, *zt"l*. He wanted to get accepted to learn in the yeshiva. The Rosh Yeshiva met him at the entrance and asked him what he was doing there. The *bachur* thought that he was one of the people who cleaned the yeshiva, so he told him that he had come to be tested to get into the yeshiva. The Rosh Yeshiva offered to help him carry his suitcase and walked with him up two flights of stairs. When they got there, the *bachur* turned to him and said, "I wonder if you can help me. You see, I brought my suitcase with me. If the person who tests me sees that I came with a suitcase, he'll think that I'm being arrogant. He may think that I brought my suitcase with me because I'm so sure that I'll get accepted, but if I leave it outside here, it could get stolen. Can you look after my suitcase while I go get tested, please?"

The Rosh Yeshiva said he would be happy to do so. The *bachur* went in, got tested, and was accepted. When he came out, he told the older man that he had been accepted. He said that they had already told him which room to go to in the dormitory. The Rosh Yeshiva happily showed him to the room. Then the *bachur* asked him, "Who are you?" The Rosh Yeshiva told him, "I'm the *shamash* of the yeshiva." The *bachur* said to him: "When I meet with the administration, I'll put in a good word for you."

After the *bachur* finished organizing his things in the room, he went down to the yeshiva. That's when he saw HaGaon Rabbi Chaim Shmulevitz sitting in the front, learning and discussing with the *bachurim*. He went over and said very excited: "Wow! The yeshiva has such amazing *shamashim*. They're so smart!" That's when some of the *bachurim* explained to him that this person was not the *shamash*; he was the Rosh Yeshiva! It was incredible to see how Rabbi Chaim Shmulevitz really cared about others.

CHALLENGE FOR THE WEEK

Let's make up a *berachah* for our brothers and sisters to do well at school.

We can also give *berachos* on birthdays and before major tests.

PARASHAS SHOFTIM

Taking Responsibility

That Friday didn't seem to be any different from other Fridays. Chaim's mother was busy cooking in the kitchen. Chaim's father had gone out to buy a few groceries that were needed urgently for Shabbos. The children were in their room, listening to an interesting story on the CD player. When the story finished, Chaim took a bath and put on his Shabbos clothes. Then he sat down to read until it would be time to go to shul.

He didn't know that his mother had gone out that morning to sort out something important at the bank and that it had taken a while, so she was running late with her preparations for Shabbos. That's why she hadn't gone into the living room in the afternoon as she always did until half an hour before Shabbos.

When she walked in, she almost fainted. "What's this? Who left his pencil box here? It's almost Shabbos! Why didn't you tidy up the Lego? And how did the comb get here? And who left the box of CDs on the table? It's muktzeh!"

Chaim's father came in to see what was going on. He was also shocked. "Chaim, all the shoes are here—why didn't you polish them yet? Who was supposed to clear the table and put the white tablecloth on? Whose job was it to tidy up the games before Shabbos? And who left his school bag here?"

Chaim felt bad. He sat down next to the pile of shoes that needed to be polished. His brothers and sisters also came running in. They were also embarrassed that they'd forgotten to do their regular chores.

The clock kept ticking. It was getting closer to Shabbos. Their mother gave a deep sigh and said, "That's how it is? If Imma doesn't remind each person about their chore, nobody does anything? Shabbos is starting in a minute and this is how we welcome her?!"

QUESTIONS FOR THE FAMILY

- Are you responsible for a specific chore at home? What is it?
- If you don't have a chore, which one would you choose?

In this week's *parashah*, it mentions that the *Kohanim* and *Levi'im* had specific times to work in the Beis Hamikdash. Moshe already divided the *Kohanim* into shifts at the time of the *Mishkan*. These shifts were called *mishmaros*. The Gemara (*Ta'anis* 27a) says that Moshe divided the *Kohanim* into eight groups: four groups of *Kohanim* from the family of Elazar the son of Aharon, and four groups from the family of Itamar, the son of Aharon. Later, Shmuel HaNavi divided them into sixteen *mishmaros*. After him, David HaMelech made twenty-four *mishmaros*. Each group worked for one week.

Why did they have *mishmaros*?

The *Sefer HaChinuch* explains as follows. If a job is given to a person or group, then it will probably get done. But if it's not clear who is

responsible for getting the job done, then very often it won't get done. Sometimes only *some* of the people will do *some* of the job, or there will be certain people who'll only agree to do a *specific* part of the work. They might feel lazy or give up and then the job will never get finished.

The topic of responsibility also shows up at the end of the *parashah*.

When a dead body is discovered, the people go and measure which is the closest city to the body. The leaders of that city have to bring an *eglah arufah* (axed calf) and say, "Our hands did not spill this blood" (*Devarim* 21:7).

This is very surprising. Would we really think that the leaders of the city are murderers? Of course not, but they *are* responsible for his death because they didn't give him food for the journey, nor did they walk with him for part of the way (Rashi ibid.).

There was once a king who was very sick. He had an extremely rare and dangerous disease. None of the doctors knew how to cure him. Then one doctor arrived and said that the king needed a very expensive medication: juice. (At that time, juice was considered a very expensive drink.) The king demanded that every family should bring him a bottle of juice by a certain date. Every family did whatever it could to buy the bottle of juice in order to save the king.

In one home, something interesting happened. The father bought a bottle of juice and put it in the cupboard. During the night, the father opened the cupboard, decided that he really wanted to taste the juice, and took a few sips from the bottle. He thought that nobody would notice if he just drank a little. The problem was that each person in the family had the same idea, and because it was dark, nobody noticed that everyone else had also drunk from the bottle.

The next day they had to take the bottle of juice to the king. When they picked up the bottle, they got a shock when they discovered that the bottle was empty! They were so scared that they didn't know what to do. Then they decided to fill up the bottle with water. They hoped that nobody would notice that they had poured water (instead of juice) into the communal barrel.

And that's exactly what they did. They brought the bottle to the palace, poured it into the communal barrel, and went home.

When the king went and took a drink from the barrel, he got a surprise. Instead of juice, the whole barrel was full of *water*! It turned out that *not one* family had brought juice to help the king get better. Everyone thought that everyone else would give the juice. In the end, no one took responsibility. The king was very angry and punished all the people.

CHALLENGE FOR THE WEEK

- Each person should try to find one thing to do to help out at home.
- Make a list of tasks that need to be done on *erev Shabbos* (or during the week) to prepare for Shabbos. Write your name next to the specific task that you'll do.

Waiting for Imma at the Meal

It was Friday night. The candles burned brightly in the shiny candlesticks. Chaim sang the Shabbos zemiros with his father and brothers.

Then it was time for the yummy Shabbos food. Their mother was in the kitchen getting everything ready to be served. The children went in and brought the different salads and special fish to the table.

Chaim's father was the first to help himself. Then all the siblings passed the food around and put the delicious fish and salads on their plates. Then they started eating.

Chaim also filled his plate. But as he was about to eat, he noticed that his mother's place was empty. She was still in the kitchen, preparing the food, organizing the dishes, and making sure that everybody got what they needed.

And what about her? When would she eat?

Imma would probably come in soon. Then she could sit down,

relax, and eat. By that time, though, everyone would've already finished the first course, so she would be the only one eating at the table.

Chaim didn't think that this was a good idea. It just didn't seem right that Imma would be the last to eat. He decided that he would wait for her this time. It wouldn't be too difficult for him to sit and wait. After all he wasn't that hungry. He'd already had a few pieces of challah.

Chaim sat and watched the rest of the family enjoying all the salads and fish that their mother had made especially for Shabbos, but he didn't take anything from his own plate.

Eventually, his mother walked into the dining room and sat down in her place. By that time, everybody else's plates were empty. She picked up her fork and began to eat.

Only after his mother started eating, Chaim picked up his fork and began to eat. The Shabbos food tasted even more delicious than usual. And it wasn't just because he was hungry. He felt so good that he had waited.

In fact, Imma noticed that Chaim had waited and thanked him. And Abba and the rest of the family saw this and decided that they would also wait for Imma from now on.

QUESTIONS FOR THE FAMILY

- Do you also wait for your mother to start to eat?
- Why is it so important to wait?

The *yetzer hara* is an angel. Chazal (*Bava Basra* 16a) say that the *yetzer hara* is the Satan, as well as the Angel of Death. This means that the being that tries to get us to sin will also prosecute us and be the one to punish us.

That doesn't sound fair, though. How can a human being fight against an angel? That's not a fair fight! Also, the angel has so much experience. He's been fighting with all sorts of people for thousands of years!

The answer lies in our *parashah*. A person's job is to go out to war and fight. If he does this, then he will get *siyata d'Shmaya*. This is what it means when it says: "When you go out to do battle with your enemy (i.e., the *yetzer hara*), Hashem will deliver him into your hand" (*Devarim* 20:1).

In the story before, Chaim wants to eat before his Imma comes back to the table. He's hungry and it's very hard for him to sit and wait. But if he decides to fight with the *yetzer hara* and tries to control himself, then he'll see that Hashem will help him to succeed.

And when he does manage to control himself, he is actually doing quite a few mitzvos. He is making his mother happy, honoring his parents, showing appreciation to his mother, caring about his mother, and working on the *middah* of being patient.

The Chazon Ish had a very special custom. Every day, he would walk to the home of his elderly mother. He would sit and talk with her for about a half an hour. The great Torah sage didn't discuss his incredible insights, Gemara topics, or halachic matters with his mother. He chatted with her about various routine affairs in order to cheer her up and make her happy.

One day, the Chazon Ish was so involved in his learning that he forgot to go visit his mother. That same day, his sister (Rebbetzin Batsheva Kanievsky, *a"h*) went to visit their mother. While they were talking, the mother mentioned that her son had not come to visit that day.

Rebbetzin Kanievsky heard this and went and told her brother, the Chazon Ish. The Chazon Ish was very upset to hear this. He got up from his seat and started to run to his mother.

Rebbetzin Kanievsky tried to run after him to calm him down, but it was no use. The Chazon Ish ran as fast as he could to his mother's home. It was as if nothing in the world could stop him. That's how important it is to show honor to parents.

CHALLENGE FOR THE WEEK

Let's try to wait until Imma comes to the table to start the meal.

Should We Worry about Getting Stung by a Bee?

A light breeze blew the snow-white festive curtains gently back and forth. The paper chains above their heads swished slightly, and the schach stirred with a gentle rustle. For Chaim, these sounds helped make Sukkos special.

The whole family sat around the beautifully laid table. They had all finished washing their hands at the portable washing station outside. They also managed to bring all the food from the kitchen on the third floor without dropping or spilling any- thing. Chaim looked around and noticed the new decoration that he had made during the last bein ha'zmanim. He really loved this chag so much!

From the sukkah next door, they could hear voices singing "V'samachta b'chagecha." Chaim's family joined in and sang the next part, "V'hayisa ach samei'ach!"

All of a sudden, the sister who was sitting closest to the door jumped up and bolted out, shrieking. The rest of the kids ran out straight after her. Their parents went out to see what happened and to help calm everyone down.

"There's a bee there!"

"It flew right over my head!"

"It landed on my cup! I wouldn't dare drink from that cup!"

One of the brothers, who was very brave, dared to peek inside and check if the cheeky intruder was still there. He looked in and got a shock. "Chaim, what are you doing here? There's a bee flying around—run away!" he shouted.

But Chaim just smiled and didn't move. He kept on reading the parashah sheet as if nothing had happened.

But then Chaim's sisters also started screaming, "Chaim, go out! The bee is right on top of you!"

"Go out?" Chaim looked up and watched the bee flying around. "What for?"

"So that you don't get stung!" yelled the frightened sisters. "It's dangerous!"

"And who says that people don't get stung outside?" asked Chaim, looking quite relaxed.

The bee looked like it was dancing around his head. "If Hashem wants the bee to sting me," explained Chaim calmly, "it won't help to run away. And if He doesn't want me to get stung, then why should I run away? It's such a pity to leave the sukkah for no reason."

QUESTIONS FOR THE FAMILY

- Do you get scared and run away when a bee comes near you?
- Do you think that a bee just stings by chance or that it stings only the person to whom it was sent to sting?

It says in the *parashah*: "And all these curses will happen to you and catch up with you" (*Devarim* 28:15).

This seems difficult to understand. If the curses will happen to a person, then obviously they will catch up with him. If so, why does the Torah add the words "and they will catch up with you?"

The answer is that even if a person tries to run away from the curses that will happen to him, it won't help—the curses will catch up to him.

From this, we can see that a bee doesn't sting by chance. It only stings the person Hashem sent it to sting.

However, this does not mean that a person is allowed to take risks or do something dangerous. In fact, the Torah obligates us to protect ourselves and to do our *hishtadlus*. For example, when riding a bike, one should always wear a helmet, and when traveling in a car, one must always wear a seatbelt.

Since remaining in the room with a bee is not risky or dangerous—and very often, a bee comes into a room, flies around, and then leaves without stinging anybody—it is appropriate to stay in the room, stay calm, and leave the bee alone.

There is one exception, though. If someone is actually allergic to bees, then it is dangerous for them to stay in a room with a bee, and the right thing for that person to do is to leave calmly and quickly.

This is an opportunity for us to strengthen our *emunah*. It's true that on Sukkos, bees may come to visit us, but if we work on our *emunah*, then we'll be able to eat happily and comfortably in the sukkah. And then the bees won't disturb our peace and quiet.

A person was once sitting and learning in the *beis midrash*. All of a sudden, a bee flew in through the window and stung him on his foot. The person who was sitting behind him in the *beis midrash* saw everything that happened. He watched the bee come in from the window on the *other* side of the *beis midrash*, fly past quite a few people, and then specifically land on this person's foot and sting him.

CHALLENGE FOR THE WEEK

This week, let's try to work on our *emunah*.

Ask Hashem each day for one thing we need—it could be a physical item or it could be help to do a mitzvah.

Speaking Gently

The ball flew straight at him. Chaim had already put his hands out to catch it, but just then, Shimon jumped in and grabbed the ball from him.

Chaim was so angry. "Thief!" he screamed. "What a chutzpah! Why'd you grab the ball from me? I had it!"

Shimon ignored him and ran away with the ball to the other side of the playground. Chaim was about to chase after him. But then he noticed the new sign on the school wall. On it was written: Always speak gently to everyone. When it was hung up a few days ago, all the children stood and stared at the big, shiny letters. Right now, though, Chaim didn't care about how it looked. He was paying attention to the actual words. That's why he stopped himself, just as he was about to carry on shouting at Shimon.

Screaming at a friend is exactly the opposite of speaking gently, thought Chaim. Still, he felt that Shimon really deserved to be shouted at! Chaim knew though that he had to control himself and try not to shout. And if he had to speak, then it had to be gently.

Chaim took a deep breath and went over to the other side of the playground. He watched the boys busy running around, playing with the ball. Then he saw Shimon run after the ball, catch it, and scream excitedly that his team won. That's when Chaim felt the anger building up in him again: How can I not say anything to him after he grabbed the ball out of my hands?

Even though it was very difficult, Chaim managed to hold himself back. He decided to rejoin the group. And from then on, he enjoyed the rest of the game.

QUESTIONS FOR THE FAMILY

- When is it difficult to speak calmly with other people?
- What would you like to work on and improve this coming year?

The Dubno Maggid explained this idea of working on oneself with a great metaphor. Imagine that there was a goldsmith who was told to come to the palace of the king. When he came, the king said to him, "I heard that you are an expert craftsman. I want you to use all of your talents to create an amazing cup for me. I want it to be the most beautiful and the most impressive cup you can design."

The craftsman's eyes lit up. This was the greatest challenge of his life—and he would get paid for it! He agreed and said, "I need a whole year to finish it. I'll need one bar of pure gold, three hundred diamonds of one carat or more, rubies, emeralds, turquoise stones, and sapphires. This is besides the salary of a hundred gold coins every month!"

The king agreed happily to everything—the gold, the diamonds, the precious stones, and even the monthly salary. After all, the royal kingdom had plenty of riches. The goldsmith started making the cup, but didn't work as hard as he could have. He didn't use all of his talents and energy to make it. Instead, he used his large salary to live extravagantly and spent it on all sorts of pleasures and luxuries. After a while, though, he needed more money to keep living like that. So what did he do? He sold some of the gold that was supposed to be for the king's cup. Then he decided to sell some of the precious stones. In the beginning, he sold only one diamond. And then another diamond. He sold more of the precious stones so that he could buy what he wanted. He partied away most of the time. When he occasionally remembered, he would spend an hour on the cup. But then he would go back to enjoying himself.

And then one day, the royal palace called to remind him. In one month, he would have to come to the king and deliver the cup that he had made.

The goldsmith got a fright. He looked at the cup and felt embarrassed. This was the magnificent cup that he had created? From a whole bar of gold?! And where were all the diamonds that he had been given? After everything, was this the cup he was able to make? Had they invited and chosen him for this? How could he give such a cheap, plain-looking cup to the king?

But he didn't give up. He thought about it and made a plan. He had another thirty days left. The gold that he had sold was gone. He also couldn't get back all the diamonds that the king had given him. But he still had the cup, even though it was quite small. He sat down and started working. He worked day and night designing the cup, making it beautiful, engraving it with beautiful outlines of roses and flowers, leaves and clusters of grapes, petals and buds. He decided that he wanted to make a cup that was one of a kind—it would be so amazing that the king would be delighted with it, and everyone would be so impressed with the king's masterpiece. He would show it off to everyone, and the king himself would boast about it and about the craftsman who made it.

He put all his effort into it. He used all his talent and all his time. He worked until the last moment; trying to add one more stunning, intricate design. On the way to the king, he polished the cup until it had a dazzling shine. When he finally presented the cup, everybody exclaimed in amazement, "This is the most impressive cup ever to be seen!"

But then the royal treasurer took the cup and weighed it. Sure enough, it was missing quite a lot of gold. He looked at it and asked, "Where are the diamonds? This is theft! You cheated the king!" The craftsman's face went white and he begged for mercy. He begged the king to forgive him for being so careless and negligent. He asked the king to save him because of all the work that he had put in and all the pleasure that the cup gave the king. All he asked for was one more chance—that he be given another year. If they would give him more gold, diamonds, and a salary, then this beautiful cup would be nothing compared to what he would make this coming year.

This is what Elul, Rosh Hashanah, and Yom Kippur are all about.

During this month, we try to change and make ourselves better than we were during the past year. We have to appear before the King and show Him all our deeds. How should we present ourselves? What should we present to Him? We are working hard to improve our ways—to purify them and upgrade them, to learn more this year, to daven with more concentration. Obviously, we cannot bring back that which was lost. We cannot make up for an entire year in one month. But we can try to improve whatever we do from now on. And then we can beg for mercy for whatever we missed out on.

Just like the modest cup, which was improved with love and personal attention, we can also improve our ways. When we polish ourselves so that we shine, we hope that we will be received favorably. Then the King will bless us with a good year.

CHALLENGE FOR THE WEEK

This week, let's try to add more mitzvos to the scale, especially by speaking nicely to everyone—no matter what happens.

PARASHAS HA'AZINU

Making Others (and Ourselves) Happy

Chaim walked to school slowly and not so happily. He had woken up late that morning and realized that his mother had already left the house. Every Monday, she left very early for work and came back very late—after he was asleep. He usually got up early on Mondays so that he could see his mother and chat with her, but this morning, he had forgotten. He had woken up early, turned over, and gone back to sleep.

He was really sad that he wouldn't be able to see or speak to his mother today. She didn't have time to answer phone calls at work. His mother had told him to call only if it was an emergency. Being sad isn't an emergency, I guess, thought Chaim.

Chaim walked into class and hung his lunchbox in its place. Even though his mother managed to make him his favorite sandwich that morning, he was still upset.

He sat down in his seat and looked around. Some kids were already on the floor, playing different games. Other boys were standing by the window and chatting. But his friend Reuven was crouching under the desk and groaning.

"What happened?" asked Chaim as he bent down to look.

"Look what happened," Reuven said as he pointed under his desk. Chaim realized immediately what happened: the shelf under the desk had collapsed. There were too many books on it and it just couldn't hold all the weight.

"Oy!" said Chaim as he looked at the nails that had bent. "It really did break. Let's see what we can do. First, let's pick up the books so that they don't just lie there on the floor. Then we'll go to Mr. Yitzchak and ask him to fix the shelf."

After they picked up the books, they went to go find the school's repairman. Chaim tried to make his friend feel better: "Don't worry—we can put some of your books on my shelf. Whatever doesn't fit, we'll leave on the desk. And Mr. Yitzchak is great at fixing these things. This happens all the time around here. It'll all be taken care of by lunchtime and you'll forget that it even happened."

Chaim really tried to make his friend feel better. And he managed. The handyman told them that he would come in a few minutes and fix it. When they got back to class, Chaim noticed that something interesting had happened. Not only had he managed to make his friend happy, but he himself had forgotten about being sad and was now in a good mood too.

QUESTIONS FOR THE FAMILY

- Do you also try to make other people happy? How?
- How do you feel when you help others?

We are about to finish reading *Chamishah Chumshei Torah* and celebrate the *chag* of *Simchas Torah*.

The Vilna Gaon once asked the Dubno Maggid why the *chag* of Simchas Torah occurs in Tishrei and not in Sivan (when the Torah was given). The Maggid answered him with a *mashal*: There was once a duke who didn't have any children. He went to get help from doctors and sorcerers, but nothing helped. His close friends and acquaintances suggested that he go to one of the *tzaddikim* of the Jewish People, who was known for doing incredible miracles. The duke came to the *tzaddik* and begged him to help. The duke also promised that he would treat the Jews well if he would have a child. The *tzaddik* prayed for the duke. A few days later, he sent the following message to the duke: "Your wife will give birth to a girl in a year from now. But it's on one condition—that your daughter never sees any man until she gets married. If she does see a man, then she'll die." Since the duke had no choice, he agreed to this difficult condition. Sure enough, when the daughter was born, the duke sent her away with a group of maids to a faraway palace. The duke's wife would often tell the duke all about how their daughter was growing up, but the duke never saw her in person. The girl grew up into a young lady and was ready to get married.

So the duke approached one of his acquaintances and asked him to let his daughter marry that person's son. But when the potential groom's father said that he would like to see the potential bride beforehand, the duke explained to him that this was impossible. The duke responded similarly to the second and third candidates to whom he wanted to marry his daughter, but nobody agreed to his terms. Eventually, he came across a lowly prince who agreed to the marriage in exchange for several precious stones and pearls that he received from the duke as a dowry. When they got married, the prince was amazed by the incredible beauty and integrity of the duke's daughter. Shortly afterward, the prince came to his father-in-law, the duke, and expressed his utmost appreciation for giving his wonderful daughter to him.

The same thing also happened to the Jewish People. Hashem offered the Torah to all the nations of the world and they didn't accept it. What did He do? He held a mountain over our heads and we accepted it involuntarily, even though we didn't know anything about it and could have thought that it wasn't worth that much.

It was only after several months went by that we found out how incredibly precious the Torah that was given to us actually was and how appropriate it was for us to rejoice over it—on Simchas Torah.

Rabbeinu Bachaya lists the mitzvah to be happy as a completely separate mitzvah from all others. This is what he says: "Because the happiness involved in doing mitzvos is a mitzvah itself." He learns this from the fact that it says: "Serve Hashem with *simchah*" (*Tehillim* 100:2).

The sefer *Chovas Adam B'olamo* (volume 5) lists two different ways that can enable a person to feel *simchah*:

1. **Doing**: There are many practical actions that help a person to feel *simchah*. For example, making another person happy, doing more of the activities that one enjoys, listening to and singing songs, etc.

2. **Thinking**: There are certain thinking exercises that create *simchah*. For example, thinking about our close relationship with Hashem, mitzvos, all the good things that Hashem gives us, etc.

CHALLENGE FOR THE WEEK

- Let's try to serve Hashem with *simchah*.
- When someone asks us to do something, let's tell him or her that we'll do it *b'simchah*!
- We can also try to make other people happy by smiling at them, treating them with respect, and taking an interest in how they're doing.

Working Together as a Family

They weren't doing anything special, just sitting down to eat supper. Chaim was the first to walk in, so he sat down in the corner on the chair without a back. Now there would be enough space on the bench for others. The older brothers huddled together and made room for their little brother. The eldest sister took her place in the big chair and put the baby on her knees. Now everybody had a seat!

Imma put a bowl of salad on the table. Chaim offered to serve. Because he was sitting in the corner, he could do so without bumping into anybody accidentally. The eldest brother passed the plate of bread rolls to whomever asked. The youngest brother, who was sitting on the edge of the bench, was the "delivery man" for everyone else. He brought a teaspoon for this one, gave a napkin to that one, passed the salt to another, and picked up a kippah when someone dropped it on the floor by mistake.

They ate calmly, shared stories, and laughed at the baby's tricks. All of a sudden, one of the boys noticed that all of them were sitting while Imma was standing.

"That's not okay!" he said and asked the sibling next to him to move for a moment so that he could get up. "Here, Imma. You can sit down. I've already finished eating."

"But you haven't bentched yet," said Imma, a little surprised.

"I'll bentch in a minute or two, when everybody else gets up, but it can't be that everybody is sitting, and Imma should be standing."

Bubby walked into the kitchen and was clearly very emotional. They were just sitting and having supper, so they couldn't understand why she was so excited. She said, "You children are fantastic! I've been standing outside the kitchen for a while already and am simply amazed by your unbelievable behavior. What incredible kids!"

The kids were very happy to hear her reaction. They just didn't understand why she was so amazed—that's how it usually was at home.

QUESTIONS FOR THE FAMILY

- Do you ever fight with anyone in your family?
- What can you do to make sure that everyone gets on with each other at home?

In this week's *parashah*, *V'zos HaBerachah*, the *pasuk* refers to Hashem when it says: "And He became King over Yeshurun [Yisrael], when the leaders of the nation got together, all of the tribes of Yisrael together."

Rashi explains: "When they get together as one unit and there is peace among them, then He is their King. And not when there is disagreement between them."

We, too, as children also need to respect each other, especially our siblings at home. That's how we'll merit to have the *Shechinah* dwell in our home.

There is a well-known story about two brothers. The oldest brother had many children while the younger brother had none.

The brothers inherited a huge field of wheat from their father. Every year, they plowed, planted, and harvested. Then they divided up the produce equally. One year, the field produced much more than it usually did. The brothers harvested the wheat and split it up equally. One brother put his share on one side of the field while the other brother put his share on the other side. When it got dark, the brothers went back to their homes. The oldest brother got into bed but couldn't fall asleep. *My poor brother,* he thought, *Hashem didn't give him any children. He and his wife are so lonely. How can I cheer them up?*

All of a sudden, he had an idea! *I'll go right now and give him some more bundles from my pile.* He got up, dressed, and went to the field. In the dark of night, he took some bundles and walked to the other side, where his brother's share was.

In the meantime, the second brother couldn't fall asleep either. *Oy, my poor brother. It's so hard for him to feed his large family,* he thought to himself. *It's really not fair to divide the harvest in half. My brother should get a much bigger share. After all, my wife and I don't need so much grain.* He decided to get up and go take some of his bundles and add them to his brother's share.

They met each other halfway. Both realized immediately what happened and hugged each other. Many years later, this place of brotherly love was where the Beis Hamikdash was built.

CHALLENGE FOR THE WEEK

Let's try and be careful to treat everyone at home with respect. This means to speak to each other respectfully, not to shout or hit, to get along with everyone peacefully, and to give in.

About the Author

DOVID SOMMER grew up in South Africa and now lives with his wife and five children in Ramat Beit Shemesh. He has taught for various Jewish youth programs from America, Australia, and South Africa and is currently teaching, writing, and translating. His specialty is translating Torah texts from Hebrew into English, with a special interest in personal growth and inspiring others to actualize their potential.

About Mosaica Press

MOSAICA PRESS is an independent publisher of Jewish books. Our authors include some of the most profound, interesting, and entertaining thinkers and writers in the Jewish community today. Our books are available around the world. Please visit us at www.mosaicapress.com or contact us at info@mosaicapress.com. We will be glad to hear from you.

MOSAICA PRESS

BOOK PUBLISHERS

Elegant, Meaningful & Bold

info@MosaicaPress.com
www.MosaicaPress.com

The Mosaica Press team of
acclaimed editors and designers
is attracting some of the most
compelling thinkers and teachers
in the Jewish community today.
Our books are available around
the world.

HARAV YAACOV HABER
RABBI DORON KORNBLUTH